The Selling Edge

How to reach the top in any sales industry

Bret J. Barrie

DEDICATION

To my beautiful, strong, brave, and brilliant wife,
Jessica. You keep our family afloat, operating, and
thriving. You're the best thing to ever happen to me,
and I couldn't imagine this life without you.

CONTENTS

ACKNOWLEDGMENTS

I want to thank all of the great mentors I've had for taking the time to show me the ropes and for the confidence you've instilled in me.

Thank you to Jesse Levine, Hal Elrod, and Adam Curchack for giving me the jumpstart I needed in my sales career. Your guidance, support, and unselfishness springboarded my career faster than anything else would have.

Thank you to Mark Karshner, Sean Welsch, and Jordan Dominic for taking a chance on me in medical sales. You guys are first-class straight-shooters, and I'm glad I didn't let you down.

Thank you to Nicole Hunt for your fantastic editing and formatting magic. It can't be easy working with a first-timer like me. You did a great job, and hopefully we can work together again on future projects.

Last and certainly not least, thank you to the members of the Golden Gate Region. You all are the best of the best, not only as professional salespeople, but also as friends. I'm honored and grateful to have worked with you all as long as we did.

INTRODUCTION

"Bret, I just don't see why anyone would spend that much money on knives. It's probably a good thing they pay you for each appointment you do." After starting my sales career with twelve unsuccessful sales pitches in a row, the final blow came from my old Little League coach.

This sales thing couldn't be that hard, could it? I was selling a good product. The knives were good. Exceptionally good! There was nothing like them on the market. The hiring manager told me there were college kids making six figures selling these knives. He also said there were students doing this part-time and making $20,000 in just one summer! So, what was I doing wrong?

Were my prospects not rich enough? Did people just not buy high-ticket items in my area? Did I have the wrong connections? Or was I just not cut out for this *sales* thing? Maybe I should just listen to my friends, who told me they didn't see me succeeding in sales, and that I was probably better suited to be a high school principal.

I've never been a natural at anything. Things just don't come as easily to me as they do to others. Growing up, I was never the best student. In elementary and middle school, I was happy with B's. Throughout high school and college, it was more of the same. I guess you could say I was better than average, but nothing special. I never got straight A's until grad school, after possessing experience in corporate America for thirteen years.

When I started playing baseball, I wasn't very good at first. In fact, at eight years old, one of my first Little League coaches told me, "You can play more when you get better." That was a tough pill to swallow for a little kid. I was undersized, weak, and a little timid.

I almost quit playing football after only two days because I was at the bottom of the depth chart. It was the same song and dance I was long used to by now. I was new to the sport, too small, and wasn't fast enough to start as a wide receiver. Thank God my dad wouldn't let me quit.

But regardless of the scenario, or how far behind the eight ball I was when starting out, I have always known how to commit to something and give it every ounce of effort I have. If I want to accomplish something, I will work relentlessly until I figure it out, and I will take action toward that goal until it starts to happen for me.

We all read the story *The Tortoise and the Hare* growing up, right? Well, I'm the tortoise. And I love being the tortoise. If I want to learn how to do something, I'll find out how others are doing it and learn what contributed to their success. Then, I'll put everything I learn into practice. Immediately and every day.

Knowing my drive and can-do attitude, I decided this sales thing couldn't be impossible. Others were achieving great things in this job. College students were making six figures doing this. Why couldn't I be one of them?

That moment was when everything changed for me.

Everything.

The thoughts I was telling myself were extremely limiting. They were based on limited information, a lack of training, and basic skill. My failure to produce results was due to my lack of experience, knowledge, and good habits. I just needed to learn a new skill set. And I did.

It came down to learning the fundamentals of sales. With any activity, there are fundamentals and best practices that put you in the best position to succeed. For any football fans, this would be the "blocking and the tackling" of selling.

The challenge I ran into, along with most people who enter their first sales job, is that there's no such thing as a natural born salesman. Boys and girls don't grow up aspiring to be professional salespeople. They grow up wanting to be doctors, dentists, lawyers, and firemen.

For most, a job in sales becomes a reality when they're fresh out of college, sleeping on their parent's couch. Sales is frequently the only job option on the table.

All companies will say they have a great sales training program. The reality is that most don't. Even if they do have a semi-decent training program, the training is frequently focused on product training and how to best pitch the products and services.

Here's the problem with that limited training. Success in sales is about getting to a decision maker, connecting with him or her, showing your value in a way that solves a problem they are dealing with, and exceeding their expectations. Long story short, the product you're selling is largely inconsequential.

It's not about you, your company, or your product. It's about the buyer.

The purpose of this book is to teach you the fundamentals and the overall process that makes a great sales person. For those who are new to sales and aspire to become top producers, this book will serve as a roadmap to help you get started. For those who are sales veterans, this book will serve as a reminder of the great habits you've built to achieve what you have. If some of those habits have faded over time, hopefully, this book can inspire you to start doing those things again and continue growing in your craft.

People come in all shapes and sizes, and salespeople are no different. No two sales people sell in the exact same way. Moreover, no two people learn and progress in the same way.

This book outlines the five absolutes every salesperson must master to be successful in sales. Just like any sport, activity, or endeavor, there are specific fundamentals that are consistent amongst the top performers. This book will show you what those fundamentals are.

Over the past 16 years, I've had the opportunity to observe and learn from some of the best sales people and sales trainers on the planet, from a multitude of industries. That experience has been both enlightening and irreplaceable and has validated to me what a "good" salesman looks like.

I've lived "in the trenches" of phone time, cold calling, networking events, dinner programs, creating interest, closing, handling objections, upselling, and asking for referrals. And did I mention the rejection of hearing the word "no" more than any other word and dealing with yelling customers?

After that day at my coach's kitchen table, I went to work. I focused on becoming a better sales person, business professional, and human being. I committed to being the best salesman I could be. I committed to devouring every bit of information I possibly could about sales, from any and every source available.

Little by little, I got better, and my numbers started to grow. I was one of the fastest reps to be inducted into the Hall of Fame with my first company, and I have achieved President's Club honors everywhere I've worked. Over the years, I have also had the pleasure of mentoring, coaching, and leading some of the top sales professionals in multiple industries.

Today, I have the honor of leading one of the top revenue-producing regions in the country within my organization, as well as the entire medical device industry. It's my opinion that some of the best sales professionals on the planet are in the medical device industry.

All kinds of people want to work in medical sales. However, few sales people have the tenacity, polish, perseverance, and grit to be successful within that space. Typically, a product in medical sales will have a minimum of four competitors, often times more. One of the products we market competes with eight other products.

Surgeons are some of the smartest customers you could ever sell to. That is a blessing, and also a curse.

You can't bullshit these people. Most of the time, they know more about your product than you do. And if they don't, they think they do. To sell in this environment, you have to be very good.

Regardless of the industry in which you sell, you must be at the top of your game. Prospects and customers nowadays know more than in any other generation. They expect more than ever before. And if you don't give them what they want, they will take their business elsewhere without hesitation.

Sales is hard. Sometimes it feels impossible. It's definitely not for everyone. But the rewards are worth it. As Tom Hopkins says, "Sales is the highest-paid hard work, and the lowest-paid easy work."

Apart from being an actor or a professional athlete, sales is the most lucrative profession on the planet - if you're good at it. Those that don't put in the work to be successful in sales will make up excuses about why the system doesn't work, how their company sucks, or how their manager doesn't give them enough training or support. At the end of the day, there's only one person who is directly responsible for your success. Just look in the mirror.

You determine how much you're worth in sales. I've always loved that no one put a dollar amount on me and told me how much they were willing to pay me. Instead, they say, this is how much we pay as a commission, now go make as much as you can. Now that's a business I want to be in!

Within the pages of this book, you will learn how to springboard you sales career faster than you ever thought possible. The practices and habits you'll learn from the teachings of this book will make you one of the best in your industry, regardless of what industry that is. If you immerse yourself in the material and implement these absolutes into your daily actions immediately, I guarantee you will see results.

While these absolutes are not original ideas, they are original in being presented in this format, with this level of simplicity. If a new idea is too difficult or too complicated to understand, I have trouble putting those items into action. When writing this book, I felt readers would feel the same. This book has been designed so you can read the idea, understand the concept behind it, and take clearly defined action steps to see results.

Additionally, each chapter recommends several pieces of work written by other authors. The books and programs referenced within these pages are some of the best books ever written on sales and personal development. To gain the maximum benefit of reading this book, I highly recommend devouring everything you can from the references included in the chapters.

There is no perfect way to do anything, and there's not a person on Earth who has all the answers. To make things easier, the recommended readings are all summarized in the back of this book. Go to Amazon.com and order all of them. If you don't, you'll miss out on valuable information that can dramatically shorten your learning curve and propel you toward the results you want much faster than by doing it through trial-and-error.

I know you're not one of those people that doesn't take action. If you were, you probably wouldn't have made it this far in the book. The worst thing that you could do is read this whole book and not put this information into practice.

Don't be one of those people!

To get the most out of this book, I have two pieces of advice.

1. Ensure you finish the book by putting a due date on it.
2. Put these practices into your daily routine immediately.

You cannot think your way to success in sales. Success in sales comes from massive action and the realization that most of these practices are not logical.

The reason most people don't achieve their goals is because they don't take enough consistent, daily actions toward reaching them. You'll read about this in Chapter 3. Instead, most people spend a lot of time thinking about achieving their goals and not enough time partaking in the activities that push them toward measurable progress in those areas.

Or even worse, many people will think up all the reasons in the world they can't accomplish a goal, and they never take action.

Anthony Robbins says, "Motion creates emotion." Sales is a momentum game, and the toughest part is getting started. Once you get the ball rolling, the game starts getting easier. Once you complete this book, you should pick up the phone, call a bunch of prospects, call some past customers, and get moving.

There's no better time to start than right now!

This trade is not impossible, although it does take work: hard work. You will have to give a greater effort than most do at their jobs. You will have to sacrifice and often times make tough decisions. You will have to tell your friends "No."

With those sacrifices, you will create abundance for yourself and your family. You will create a lifestyle you can be proud of, a life that allows you to provide your family the things money can buy, and most importantly, the things money *can't* buy.

Let's get started on the path. Thank you for choosing this book and allowing me to play a small role in your success as a salesperson. I'm confident you won't be disappointed. For those willing to put in the hard work, log the long hours, and shed the blood, sweat, and tears, I'm happy to share with you *The Selling Edge*.

Enjoy!!!

"Today I will do what others won't, so tomorrow I can accomplish what others can't."
~ Jerry Rice

MENTORSHIP

I knew it couldn't be impossible to succeed in this wild world of sales. If others were achieving the accolades I desired, I knew I could do it too. Although I didn't understand this world at the time, I knew the resources were there, the training was there, and most importantly, the opportunity for me to succeed was there.

I soon realized there were several things I did not know about sales. So, I started thinking of how I could figure them out. If others were already figuring this game out, I wondered if they would be willing to share some tips and tricks they'd learned with me. In this world, asking others for the answers to the test wasn't going to be a bad thing, and I soon realized that was where I needed to start. I could keep beating my head against a wall and hope that I figure it out on my own. But I remembered my college baseball coach used to recite the Albert Einstein quote, "Insanity is doing the same thing over and over, and expecting a different result."

I was like a fly trapped inside a car with the

windows rolled up that keeps flying into the window, trying to get out. At least my sales habits and practices were like the fly.

If I continued working at this rate, or harder, and taking more of the action that was leading away from success, I would just fail faster. Around that time, I went to my first division meeting.

For those who have never been to a sales meeting before, it feels like you're joining a cult. Parents and outsiders especially start to believe that. Sales reps show up with notepads, tape recorders, and positivity that would scare even the slightest pessimist away in a single heartbeat.

In the case of my first-ever Vector Marketing Division Meeting, the meeting changed my life, and the cult leader ended up becoming one of the best mentors of my career.

Jesse Levine has a personality. A HUGE personality. He shook my hand with a huge grin and unrelenting eye contact, and said, "You're Bret Barrie? I've heard great things about you. Your manager has already told me all about you. It's a pleasure to meet you! I'm glad you could make it to the meeting tonight!"

Was this the Vector Marketing version of David Koresh? Was I being sucked into the cult? Was the first item on the agenda to start downing the Kool-Aid? Regardless of what this weird world of positivity was, there was something that told me I was in the right place. I didn't know what it was, but I picked a seat in the front row and decided to listen with an open mind, take good notes, ask questions, and try to learn this sales thing.

Within the first five minutes of the meeting, Jesse

was talking about associations and the people you hang out with. And then he said the quote I've never forgotten. The famous business philosopher Jim Rohn said, "You are the average of the five people you spend the most time with."

In essence, you are your associations. It reminded me of the time in 8th grade that my basketball coach called my mom and told her I was hanging out with troublemakers on the playground at lunchtime. These kids were starting to dabble in drugs, girls, and dangerous activities. But I wasn't involved in any of the shenanigans, and I pleaded my case to my mom.

My mom said to me, "It doesn't matter if you're doing the things they are or not. If you are hanging out with those kids, everyone will assume you are, regardless. Because birds of a feather fly together."

The people we spend time with leave an impression on us. Over time, we start to take on their traits, beliefs, habits, and actions. The things they consider normal, we start to think are normal as well. The standards they have for themselves, we will start to adopt for ourselves. Conversely, if they have low standards and productivity and aren't perceived in a positive light, those traits will rub off on us as well.

Sitting there in 2001, listening to Jesse Levine talk about associations and the value of learning from others who have been successful, was the most impactful thing I have ever experienced. Sales wasn't impossible, and I could figure it out. Not only could I figure it out, but I was determined to become one of the best in this industry.

It was simple. I needed to make friends with some top achievers, look for ways I may be able to add value to their business, and see if they would take me under their wings. Now, I just needed to find out who those people were.

Throughout that first meeting, several up-and-coming representatives gave presentations to the group of new hires, sharing with us the best practices that contributed to their early success. I took notes feverishly, swallowing up everything they had to share. I still have my notes to this day.

After that meeting, I went home and reviewed my notes. There was so much great information, and I realized if I didn't figure out how to put it into practice immediately, it would be useless.

That night I stayed up until 3 a.m. looking back at each of my first 12 appointments that resulted in no sales, replaying each of those appointments in my mind. Specifically, I looked at what went well, the areas in which I needed to improve, and what actions I could take differently in the future to produce a better result.

The next morning, I woke up with a greater sense of confidence. Although I was still a little apprehensive, I felt like I had a better understanding of what I needed to do to generate results. Using some of the new skills I'd learned, I started making phone calls to schedule more appointments.

The next day, implementing the new tips and tricks I'd learn at the meeting, I made three sales in five appointments. The thought that someone had bought something as a result of my efforts alone gave me a thrill that I hadn't felt since hitting in the winning run in a high school baseball game. I knew if I had done it once, I could do it again!

Over the next month, I continued working on my skills, and I committed to completing at least ten appointments per week. Although my skills seemed to be improving, and my results definitely were, I knew I had a long way to go before I could call myself a salesman.

About six weeks from my first Division Meeting, we had our first summer conference, where all the representatives and managers from the Western Region got together to recognize top performers and to share best practices. When my manager informed us of the upcoming summer conference, he gave us an informational brochure as well. The front of the brochure listed the information about the conference.

However, when I turned the brochure over, the sales standings for the Western Region, and also for the entire nation, were listed on the back. Several of the names in the standings were some of the reps Jesse had referenced during the division meeting.

That night I set a goal to meet at least three of the top reps at the conference. Specifically, I wanted to make a connection and pick their brain during the meeting. I also wanted to try to exchange contact information with them. So, during the conference, I did just that.

What I found was life changing. While I was a little apprehensive to approach these top reps at first, I found them all to be very approachable, extremely receptive, and eager to share their tips, tricks, and strategies that had contributed to their own success.

That day in 2001, I met one of my earliest mentors who made a huge impact on my early selling career, "Yo Pal" Hal Elrod.

Hal was one of the top reps in Fresno, just a couple hours south of the Sacramento area. We were first introduced by Jesse during that summer conference, and I latched on immediately. Hal had been with the company for a few years and was one of the top reps in the nation. More remarkable, however, was Hal's story and the challenge and adversity he had overcome to become successful at Vector.

Two years before, in 1999, Hal was driving home one evening after speaking at a division meeting in Modesto and was hit head on by a drunk driver. His heart stopped for six minutes; he sustained numerous fractures throughout his body, and he was told he'd never walk again. After a lengthy recovery, Hal defied all odds and was back working passionately toward his goals. It appeared that he refused to let anything get in his way, even a life-altering accident!

After a great conversation at the summer conference where Hal shared with me some of his best strategies for setting appointments and generating more customer referrals, I knew the information I had gathered was just a fraction of what I could learn from him. At the end of our conversation, I asked Hal if we could exchange numbers and if I could call him to pick his brain periodically, which he graciously agreed to.

Six months and 50 phone calls later, he probably regretted giving me his number, although Hal has never admitted to that. During that time, Hal and I had conversations about almost everything, not just selling. I will forever be indebted to Hal for all of his wisdom and guidance, even to this day.

Hal has gone on to become an international best-selling author, motivational speaker, podcast host, personal and business coach, and an incredible husband, father, and friend. When my wife and I got married in 2011, Hal got ordained as a minister and officiated our wedding ceremony. For those who would like the opportunity to learn from Hal, you can find his work at halelrod.com.

Another practice that catapulted my sales career was what the people at Vector Marketing call "field training," where reps tag along on sales calls and watch other reps handle their appointments. Essentially, it's like being a fly on the wall during a presentation.

When I first started at Vector, field training was something that newer reps did to learn from the veteran reps. It was extremely beneficial. This practice became so helpful that over time even veteran reps chose to field train with one another. To this day, I encourage my sales team to field train together, regardless of their experience level. Field training is the quickest way to shorten the learning curve and increase confidence, especially when it comes to increasing your effectiveness in sales appointments.

Learning new information in a conference is fantastic, and I've learned a ton of great tips and best practices through listening to presenters. However, there is always a gap that just doesn't feel real, with a certain level of ambiguity. When it comes to field training, there is none of that. You get to see it with your own two eyes, and you get to feel it because you're sitting right there in the room with the salesperson and the prospect.

Imagine hearing Michael Jordan discuss how to play basketball. He could tell you all about the correct fundamentals, mindset, and ways to create an opening to shoot the ball. He could also explain how to guard another player and how to successfully rebound a ball

BRET J. BARRIE

from another player on the court. There would certainly be value in that.

Now imagine playing basketball with Michael Jordan and learning all these movements from him while he demonstrated to you how to do them. Instead of telling you how to shoot a ball, he could show you how to shoot it. Instead of telling you how to box someone out and grab a rebound, imagine how much clearer it would be to watch him do it live. Also, imagine how much better you'd understand the grit, tenacity, and can't-lose attitude of Michael Jordan if you actually watched it unfold in front of your own two eyes. It makes a real impact, and it gives you confidence that you can do it too. That's field training.

The most impactful field training experience I've ever had in my career came roughly a year after I met Hal when I was introduced to another CUTCO legend, Adam Curchack. Adam started with Vector in the Santa Rosa, California area and, after crushing it for several years, decided to open a Vector branch office in Honolulu, Hawaii. After Adam realized he liked the freedom and flexibility of being a sales rep more than a manager, he decided to step down from running the office, although he continued selling Cutco in Hawaii for a couple more years. During that time, he was one of the first reps to win the GMT Master II Oyster Perpetual Rolex the company awards to top sales people, and he was also one of the fastest to reach the company's storied Hall of Fame.

Adam decided to relocate back to Northern California, where I met him in the spring of 2002. After speaking at a local division meeting, Adam and I were introduced through Jesse and Hal. Adam and I hit it off immediately, and after a long conversation that evening, I asked Adam if I could drive out to Santa Rosa and field train with him for a day, which he agreed to.

So I drove out to Santa Rosa on a random Wednesday in the summer of 2002 and watched Adam do four appointments with prospects. Adam was good. Very good.

When I watched the way he presented the product to the customer, he seemed to have a deeper level of connection with the customer than what I had. They seemed to feel completely comfortable with him, and he was completely comfortable with them. There was no awkwardness or weirdness like my presentations sometimes had. Midway through one of the presentations, I remembered thinking, "This is how it would feel if you were presenting these products to your best friend's Mom." Effortless.

It was obvious that Adam had done hundreds of presentations over the years. His talk tracks were clean, crisp, and oozed with confidence. When the customer asked a question regarding the product or voiced a concern about moving forward in the buying process, Adam's answers carried much more conviction than mine did at the time.

In the car between appointments, I asked Adam hundreds of questions around his business. How do you organize your leads? When do you do phone time? How many calls do you make when you do phone time? What do you do if a customer doesn't want to give you referrals?

By the end of the day, Adam was probably sick of me. However, what I realized is he was doing all the same things I was doing, except his messaging was crisper and more confident, and he was taking more action than I was. MUCH MORE.

When answering the questions around phone time, Adam's answers were: he does phone time whenever he's working and not on an appointment, and he makes as many calls as necessary to get the appointments filled. According to Adam, it wouldn't be uncommon for him to make 100 to 200 phone calls to prospects in one sitting.

As I was looking over my notes that evening and reflecting on the day together, two things become very clear to me. I went through my calendar from the prior four months and averaged out how many appointments I was doing per week.

When I averaged them out, I realized I was only doing 7.4 appointments per week. Adam was averaging anywhere from 15-20. Based on my averages (closing percentage and average order), if I could increase the number of appointments I was doing, my sales would increase exponentially.

The other key takeaway was the overall belief Adam had in the products, the company, and most importantly, himself. He didn't walk into any of the appointments wondering *if* the customer would buy. The only question he had was *what* the customer would buy. He believed in the products and his ability to demonstrate them so well that the thought of someone not buying from him didn't even cross his mind.

An important note about field training with a mentor: do not say a word in the appointment. You are a fly on the wall. When your mentor walks up and meets his or her prospect, let them introduce you, and then leave it at that. Let them do the presentation.

Staying completely silent can be difficult even for newer reps, especially if you notice you have something in common with the prospect that would be easy to talk about. However, resist the temptation! Let the mentor conduct the presentation. If the prospect, or even your mentor, turns and asks you a direct question during the appointment, obviously it's okay to answer it. However, simply answer the question and then let the conversation shift back to your mentor and the prospect.

I greatly appreciate the mentorship of Jesse, Hal, Adam, and many others during my days selling CUTCO, and my yearning to be mentored by those who are successful hasn't stopped. It never should.

You cannot reach the pinnacle of success as quickly, and your potential will be limited, without great mentors. As you progress through your career, you will need to adjust your mentors, based on your experience, skills, and aspirations.

When you find a mentor, here are the best tips for working with them:

1. Define the relationship – It's important to create proper expectations for what you are looking to get out of the interactions, and vice-versa.

2. Define boundaries – How often will you speak? Will you work together in person, by telephone, or FaceTime? This was an area I abused when I first started working with mentors, and I want to make sure you don't make the same mistake.

3. Define follow-up action items to be completed between interactions – The best way to capitalize on new information learned is to

implement it immediately. Jeffrey Gitomer says, "Knowing and doing are not the same." Truer words were never spoken.

4. <u>How can the mentee add value to the mentor?</u> – Is there a way the mentor can learn or gain something from the mentee? Also, what requirements or requests does the mentor have in order to make working together beneficial for him or her? The relationship should not be one-sided, and the mentee should look for ways to add value to the mentor.

5. <u>How will accountability be measured?</u> – Mentoring someone is a huge undertaking and involves a significant time commitment. Also, it's a commitment from the mentee to allow someone the opportunity to teach him. How will both be held accountable to ensure the relationship and the quality of interactions exceed both party's expectations?

Working with mentors is career changing, and also life changing. Also, as you progress throughout your sales career, a new representative seeking good counsel will undoubtedly approach you for your wisdom.

Be a mentor. Teach them all you can.

Every time.

Regardless of what you may have to juggle around in your schedule to make it work, do it. While this may seem counterintuitive, the person who benefits the most from a mentorship relationship is the mentor.

Yes, that's right. The mentor benefits the most.

You might be thinking, "No way! How can that be if the mentee is the one receiving new information?"

According to the late American psychiatrist William Glasser, we retain:

10% of what we read

20% of what we hear

30% of what we see

50% of what we see and hear simultaneously

70% of what we discuss

80% of what we experience

95% of what we teach others

So when you're a veteran rep and someone new approaches you and wants to pick your brain, it's important to remember a couple of things. For one, you had mentors who helped you along when you were new, so you should pay that back in the effort of helping others become successful in sales. Secondly, mentoring someone new is one of the key strategies for improving your existing skills. You never know who that person is, and more important, who they could become. Of all the accolades and awards I've ever earned from my time in sales, the ones I relish the most involve the success of other people I've mentored and coached.

When someone approaches you, remember, there's always a chance that person could be your boss someday!

You might be saying to yourself, "Yeah Bret, that sounds great. But I don't have anyone around me that would be a good mentor for me…"

I would respectfully challenge that notion.

Sure, interpersonal relationships and dealings with others are probably the most conventional, and also most considered mentor relationships. However, in the information era that we live in, there are mentors all around you!

Here are additional sources for your learning and growth:

Books
Audio CDs
Webinars
TED Talks
YouTube
Podcasts on iTunes
Seminars

The great thing about most of these resources is that you can get them for free (providing you have a smartphone) or for a very small investment. Three months ago, podcasts wouldn't have even been on this list (I know, I'm a little behind in the times). However, I've recently realized there are some amazing podcasts with interviews and expert opinions, on just about anything!

Just to share a tidbit of information, I've recently come across a FANTASTIC sales-training podcast called *The Advanced Selling Podcast* with Bill Caskey and Bryan Neale. It's the longest-running sales-training podcast on iTunes, and each week they dive into a different area of sales, often interviewing successful salespeople, coaches, and entrepreneurs. I highly recommend it, and it's free!

The late Charlie "Tremendous" Jones used to say, "You will be the same person in five years as you are today except for the people you meet and the books you read." If there's a topic you want to learn something about or become great at, odds are there are over 100 books written on the subject.

Furthermore, there are great sources out there in addition to great books. The information is out there. The two questions I have for you are:

1. How hard are you willing to look for it?
2. What will you do once you find it?

"You are the average of the five people you spend the most time with."

~ Jim Rohn

CONNECTION

Who's the greatest salesperson you've ever met? When you think of a great sales person, and the traits and personality exemplified by that person, what thoughts come to mind?

Most people would say that the person has "the gift of gab," he's a "talker," a "charmer," he's got "a way with words," or even, "he's just a natural-born salesman!"

To put that notion to rest, there's no such thing as a "natural born salesman." However, some people's personalities are more naturally predisposed to being conversational, outgoing, and easy to talk to. When I started out in sales, I definitely didn't fit into that mold. It's something I continue to work on today.

Regardless of what you want to call it, the real word those people are looking for is "connection." Top salespeople, and most leaders in every industry for that matter, have the ability to connect with others in a way lower-producing individuals simply cannot.

The most important aspect of sales is getting someone's attention and connecting with them on a level where they feel compelled to hear what you have to share with them. It's obviously more complex than that, and if it weren't, there'd be no need for books like this. However, the sales process really can't start until you can connect with prospects and customers on a level where they want to hear what you have to say.

One of the greatest connectors I've ever met was the guy who recruited me into medical sales, Mark Karshner. Mark had been wildly successful in medical sales as a sales rep, national sales trainer, and a regional Director of Sales.

When I first interviewed with Mark, I was apprehensive about working with a new manager and a new company. After my success with Vector, and the great relationship I'd had with Jesse and everyone there, I didn't know how I'd adjust to a new company and culture.

Mark eliminated all doubt in an instant.

The first time I met Mark in person was during my initial interview, on a park bench in Union Square in San Francisco in 2006. Mark's a pretty casual guy, and it made me drop any wall whatsoever.

From the second we sat down, I knew I wanted to work with this guy. Initially, I noticed his handshake. It was a confident, firm, handshake that led me to believe he was a stand-up guy.

Within five minutes, he'd already asked me two or three things about myself. No questions whatsoever about the job, my qualifications, or any of that stuff.

He wanted to know about me and who I was.

And I noticed, as I shared my story with him, he maintained an unwavering eye contact, leading me to trust him.

It was very apparent that he was a positive, upbeat, energetic guy who was an opportunity thinker. He was passionate and exuded an energy level and a zest for life that few others demonstrate, much like Jesse had demonstrated several years before.

Sure, Mark wanted to discuss the requirements of the position and if I'd be a good fit, and we definitely did that day. But he would always bring the conversation back to me, and what was best for me.

I literally felt like, even though I was just another interviewee, that I was his #1 customer. Even though I had just met the guy, there wasn't a doubt in my mind I could work well with him.

At the end of that interview, I had no reservations about joining the company. He had connected with me, and within two weeks he offered me an opportunity to join his sales team.

I will forever be indebted to Mark for giving me the opportunity in medical sales. While many new hires in medical sales already possess medical or healthcare experience, I didn't.

However, Mark saw in me something that I, at the time, didn't even see in myself, and he connected with me well enough to convince me to take the plunge.

That was one of the best decisions of my life.

Shifting gears back toward sales and connecting with customers, your customers should feel comfortable sharing anything with you about their business, their family, and their interest level in your products or services. They should feel comfortable disclosing any competitive options they may be considering, or even taking their business elsewhere, without feeling that you'll pull a fast one on them.

If you feel the sense that you aren't getting the

whole story from a customer, you aren't fully connected with him or her. They most likely don't trust you, and they also don't feel like you have their best interest in mind.

Do you want a good test to find out how well you're connecting with your prospects and customers? Two areas in the selling process that will give you a very accurate reading are when it comes to the point in the appointment where the customer is going to buy or not, and when it comes time to ask them to refer you to friends, family, and colleagues.

If you have built a solid rapport level with the customer, and they have concerns or questions regarding your product or service, they will feel comfortable expressing those concerns honestly and directly. The point in the appointment where you ask them if they're ready to buy, or if they want to get started, or however you ask for the order, is where the true test arises.

A few years ago, a former colleague of mine encountered a prospect who is an orthopedic surgeon and a perfect fit for our products. He liked the product we offered, had experience using it during his training in residency, and treated several patients per month that were great candidates for it. However, he never bought from her. Furthermore, he didn't even buy from any of our competitors, either.

Several years ago, my colleague moved on to a different venture, and our manager at the time re-aligned the territory. My manager backfilled the position with a new representative who was much more personable than my former colleague. About three weeks after the new rep started, I saw this particular physician's name show up on our billing list. I asked my new colleague what she did to get the doctor's business, because he hadn't ordered from us ever before, over a very long period of time.

She said, "Well, I went in and met with him and his staff. We had a great meeting, and they are a great group of people. By the end of the lunch, they were stocking the shelves with our product. When I asked them why they never ordered from the former rep, they said they always felt like she was more interested in her commission and that she wasn't really there to help them and their patients."

Obviously, this particular customer felt much more comfortable opening up to their new rep they had known for 30 minutes than they felt with the previous rep who called on them for several years. Sometimes the sales cycles for products can be tedious and time-consuming, but often times, the connection with a customer or prospect can happen in an instant.

Another point in the sales process that clearly reveals the level of rapport a rep has with a customer is when the rep asks the customer for personal referrals, which all sales people should do. If a customer hasn't been made to feel comfortable by the salesperson, the common answer is "Oh, I don't do that to my friends."

Don't do what?

I remember being new in sales and thinking, "Well geez! Was I THAT bad that sitting and talking to me for a few minutes and taking a look at something that might make your life a little easier make your friends hate you forever?" Of course not.

However, they didn't know that at the time, and I hadn't done a good enough job of connecting with them in a way where they felt comfortable referring me to their friends. That's really what they were saying. I just hadn't made them feel comfortable enough for them to express it honestly.

When customers feel connected to you and feel like you have their best interest in mind, they will bend over backward to help you out. They'll buy everything they possibly can, they'll switch their schedule around to help accommodate your schedule, they'll refer you to all their friends and colleagues, and they'll even invite you to family gatherings.

One of the most fulfilling experiences I ever had as a rep was when my #1 customer discovered that I had coached high school baseball for eight years at a Northern California high school well known for its baseball success. It just so happened that this customer's two sons, who were eight and ten at the time, were really into baseball and played year round. After about three years of working with this surgeon, he told me how he was coaching his sons' Little League team and was curious if I'd be willing to do a clinic for all the players.

I certainly wasn't going to tell my top customer no, especially when it was something in my wheelhouse that I could easily help him with. However, I was elated that he felt comfortable enough with me that he'd invite me to not only help out the Little League team he was coaching, but most of all, he felt comfortable with me coaching his own children.

When your customers invite you into their family, that's the ultimate feedback where you, as a salesperson, know you are doing a great job. At that point, you aren't a salesperson to that customer anymore.

You are a valuable resource for them, a trusted advisor, and, more importantly, a friend.

Here are five tips for building better connections:

1. Read Dale Carnegie's *How to Win Friends and Influence People* at least once a year – first published in 1936, this book has now sold over 15-million copies worldwide and is still one of the best-selling personal development books year-over-year.

2. Keep stronger eye contact – Shakespeare said, "The eyes are the window to the soul." Studies have shown for hundreds of years that people who make and maintain stronger eye contact are more likeable, more trustworthy, and have greater influence over others than people who don't.

3. Learn people's names, and remember them! – Dale Carnegie says a person's name is the most important word to them in the whole world. If that's true, and you're trying to connect with someone you've just met, remembering his or her most important word is a great start.

4. Listen twice as much as you speak – especially when meeting someone for the first time, it's easy to fill the silence by telling that person all about you. The best communicators ask questions and get the other person to talk about him or herself. If you need help starting or keeping a conversation, remember the 5 P's (people, pets, pictures, plants, and places). Ask about these five things, and you can keep people talking for hours!

5. Listen to understand, not to respond – the late Dr. Stephen Covey used to say, "Most people

do not listen with the intent to understand; they listen with the intent to reply." This is extremely difficult to do, and it's something I'll be working on until my own dying day. A good strategy that helps in this area is something I learned in a leadership training class several years ago: "Listen 'til the last drop." Good luck with that!

5 books to read on building better connection:
1. *How to Win Friends and Influence People* – by Dale Carnegie
2. *Love is the Killer App* – by Tim Sanders
3. *The 5 Love Languages* – by Gary Chapman
4. *Emotional Intelligence* – by Daniel Goleman
5. *The Likeability Factor* – by Tim Sanders

"Most people do not listen
with the intent to
understand; they listen with
the intent to reply."
~ Stephen R. Covey

PLANNING

There's an old saying, "If you fail to plan, you plan to fail." No place is this truer than in the world of sales, where quotas must be met, existing customers need service, sales managers want business plans and reports, and oh, yeah... you have to find more prospects to buy your product or service.

Across all industries of selling, the highest producing sales reps manage their business and manage their schedule, while the representatives who don't perform as well allow their schedule and their business to manage them. That's much easier said than done.

Many sales people feel like when they're working they would rather enjoy time with friends and family, and when they're not working, they feel guilty that they're not working. If you've been in sales for any length of time, I'm sure you've felt the same way.

So how do you fix this? The answer lies in a sales person's ability to plan his schedule and then work that plan in a disciplined manner over an extended period.

What I'm about to teach you is something I learned from an old mentor of mine. To give proper credit where it's due, he originally learned it from Tony Robbins. It's called "The Hour of Power."

My rendition of the Hour of Power consists of setting aside one hour per week to focus strictly on planning. All other distractions and priorities are set aside, and the sole focus is on firming up the next week, and then loosely planning the three weeks after.

Turn off your email, Facebook, and cell phone. If you work in an office where interruptions are likely to occur, go to a quiet coffee shop for an hour. Also, trying to do this at home, with kids running around and screaming won't work either.

To make this exercise most beneficial, you must have complete silence and the chance to sit and think.

The best time to do the Hour of Power is usually Thursday or Friday. If you wait until Monday morning to plan your week, you won't start the week quickly enough to achieve the great results you're looking for.

Instead, you'll get up Monday morning, read some sales reports, get engulfed in emails that weren't handled the week before, return a couple of client calls, and get your Monday morning call from your sales manager to "motivate" you. These distractions don't align with your sales goals.

Here's what happens: you do all of those things, and before you know it, it's noon on a Monday, and you've spent half of one of the key selling days of the week doing a bunch of non-selling activities.

Hundreds of articles and books have been written on the importance of getting up early and the benefits of getting a great start to the day. When it comes to sales, momentum plays a huge factor in your level of success. Getting a sale first thing on Monday morning is the best way to get your week off to a great start!

Tom Hopkins says that in sales, "Working is only the time you spend in front of a qualified prospect. Everything else is preparation for work." Keeping this is mind, you wouldn't want to waste a Monday morning of sales potential, simply because the planning wasn't done ahead of time.

The specific time of day that you do your Hour of Power doesn't matter. What's important is that you set aside at least an hour of time each week to solidify next week's plan and to loosely start mapping out the following three weeks.

Having a detailed schedule mapped out before the week starts will get you off to a quicker start, will create more focus and clarity in your targeting, and will allow you to run a PROACTIVE business, not a REACTIVE one.

Most sales people react to what happens to them. High-achieving sales people take charge and make their day and week unfold how they want it to.

Let's talk about the specific steps to putting your schedule together. Grab out your planner or calendar for next week, and let's get started!!!

#1 – Personal / Free Time

You might find it odd that this is the first thing to put it in the schedule. However, let me ask you a question.

When you fly on an airplane, and the flight attendant gives the warning message at the beginning of the flight, whose mask does she say to put on first? The answer is obvious, especially for those who have flown a significant number of times.

She says to put your own mask on first.

What would happen if you put on the masks of the people around you first and put your own mask on last? It sounds less selfish, right? It sounds like you're a great, unselfish person who will put others' needs before your own.

Let me phrase it a different way. What happens if you put two of the people's masks on and before you can get to the third person next to you, who happens to be a child, you drop dead? That's correct. Two of the four people you are trying to save, including yourself and a child, die.

Now, what happens if you put your mask on first? Obviously, you would then be able to have the strength and capability to put on the other three people's masks. You'd be able to put on as many masks for others as you needed to. Now how many people die? Zero.

See my point?

By taking care of your needs first, you are now stronger and more able to take care of the needs of others. Also, you're in a better frame of mind to handle the adversity and challenging aspects of sales and everything that goes into selling. I know this may be a disastrous and completely unreasonable example, but I wanted to make sure and get your attention around this point.

If you don't get your mind, body, and spirit right, and if you're not healthy mentally, physically, and emotionally, you won't be your best to take care of everyone and everything you need to in your life.

So, what are the personal/free time items that need to be put in your schedule first? For most people, it would be things like working out, writing or journaling, reading, meditating, personal/professional development courses or seminars, doctors' appointments, and church or another spiritual activity.

If you have children, I would include your children's important activities here as well, such as school plays, Christmas programs, Little League or soccer games. You could even factor in helping your kids with homework or having quality "fun time."

Today, kids need parental support and guidance more than ever. If you're organized and disciplined, there is enough time in the day to accomplish everything you need to.

Regardless of how busy or stressful things get at work, don't neglect your kids and family because of it. Get better at making it all work.

If you have a spouse or significant other, make sure to schedule a date night or a date-type activity once every week. When work gets busy and kids get wrapped up in school and after-school activities, and everything else that has to be done during a week, it's easy for the time you spend alone with your significant other to suffer. Don't let this happen!

What's the point in making a bunch of money if you lose your family in the process? Then you're just rich and lonely. I don't know about you, but I'd rather be doing pretty well and have a loving spouse and family than be crazy rich and lonely.

Work will always be there. Your children won't always be the age they are now, and they won't be in the house forever.

I get it. It's tough, and sometimes it feels impossible to balance all of the competing priorities. Just remember: someday, your kids will be grown up and gone.

You'll want your relationship with your spouse to be stronger than ever. The reasons why this happens are definitely beyond the true scope of this book, but the reality isn't.

Don't let work run your life. Take time to love and support the ones you're working hard for. It's a tough balance, but with sound planning and discipline, you can do it.

There are a ton of different activities that would fit into this category, and probably far too many to label all of them in this chapter. The important thing to remember is these are activities that will improve your mental, physical, and emotional health, and the lives of those around you.

Are there times that come up where your personal schedule conflicts with you work schedule? Of course! This probably happens more often than not. However, the beauty of being in sales is, for the most part, you get to create your own schedule.

Are there times when you may have to miss one of your kids' Little League games because of a work meeting? Sure. That's definitely a possibility. Sometimes, there's just nothing you can do, and you can't beat yourself up over it. However, you have to be honest with yourself, and your family, and ensure it doesn't happen very often.

Once you have your personal time and obligations scheduled for the week, it's time to move onto the next step.

#2 - Corporate Obligations

This is where you enter anything that's assigned to

you by the company. These might be sales meetings, conference calls, webinars, or meetings with your manager.

There's really not much explanation needed to show the importance of this one. Basically, if you work for a company and the company has scheduled meetings, you have to attend them. However, by mapping your week out ahead of time, if there are any scheduling conflicts that arise, you will have the time to proactively handle them.

If you do realize that the scheduling conflict exists, the best thing to do is talk to your manager or supervisor about it ahead of time. Often, a superior will be able to advise you accordingly.

If she feels the meeting is not as important to attend as the other item in your calendar, she may give you a pass for the meeting. However, managers aren't as excited when they get a call five minutes before a scheduled meeting that one of their direct reports has a scheduling conflict.

This recently happened to me. My wife and I were due with our third child four weeks after my company's annual national sales meeting. We were pretty sure the baby wouldn't be born while I was at the meeting.

However, we weren't 100% positive, and her OB/GYN recommended I not make the trip halfway across the country to San Antonio so close to our due date, just in case. While I was a little nervous about approaching my boss, I did approach him with it.

Long story short, he was in full support of me staying home with my wife and family during that time and because I brought it to him a full eight weeks before the sales meeting, we were able to plan accordingly for my absence. As much as I hate to say it, I don't think they missed me at all.

When this topic comes up, I always remember playing sports in high school and college. Away games and road trips for baseball would require missing a class, and often times, several classes.

Our coaches always recommended that we go to our professors during their office hours at the beginning of the semester to discuss any sports-related obligations that might conflict with their class, especially any assignments or tests that might be due during a time we were away on a road trip.

The outcome was pretty simple. The players who approached their professors proactively always seemed to end up with satisfactory grades in the class. However, the players who waited until the night before a test to inform the instructor (if they told her at all!) didn't seem to do as well.

The solution is pretty obvious. By scheduling and planning ahead, you have the opportunity to discuss any potential conflicts with your supervisor and get her feedback and advice on the matter as well. If you're PROACTIVE, the outcome will almost always be in your favor.

#3 - Customer-Requested Appointments

Customer-requested appointments involve those appointments with top prospects or customers where they have asked you to meet with or call them at a certain time. Usually, these appointments involve a top prospect or high-value customer, and the customer does not have much flexibility in his schedule.

With these scenarios, it's pretty simple. If you want the business, you'll show up at the requested time. There are several examples that come to mind.

In consumer-type sales, or what is called business-to-consumer (B to C), frequently the best chance of success is when both spouses are present during the sales presentation. From my days selling CUTCO, I remember the difference in results when I did a sales presentation for one spouse alone versus when both spouses were present.

When meeting with both spouses, the percentage of appointments where I made a sale and my average order size were both significantly higher. When meeting with one spouse alone, that spouse would usually want to wait and run the purchase by the other spouse when they got home. And even though our strategies would usually convince the first spouse to at least order something, the average order was much smaller, and so was the closing percentage.

By the end of my time at CUTCO, I realized that it was worth it to schedule the majority of my appointments during evenings and weekends when the likelihood of both spouses being present for a presentation drastically increased.

This scenario occurs across the entire selling industry. For someone selling cars, a hot prospect or loyal customer may want to schedule a test drive when she is off work for the day. Someone buying a house will most likely want to meet with her realtor when she and her husband are off work.

Having several friends in the real estate industry, I can tell you sales people in that industry achieve some of their best results working in the evenings and weekends as well.

In medical device sales, a physician or surgeon will want to use a product on a patient, and the patient is scheduled for a surgery or a clinic appointment at a pre-scheduled time.

It is imperative for sales people not to miss these opportunities. In most cases, customer-requested appointments with qualified prospects generate extremely powerful results.

#4 – Prospecting/Scheduling Calls

To achieve a high level of success in sales, you must always be "hunting" for new prospects and continuously scheduling appointments to present your products or service to them. Prospecting calls can be scheduled in person, over the phone, and via electronic channels as well.

Industry norms, time, and geography of your territory all affect which medium is most effective to schedule appointments with prospects.

When I was selling CUTCO, we did what we called "Phone Time," where we made dozens of calls to schedule appointments with qualified prospects for the upcoming week or two. In my experience, most selling methods work in this fashion, where the sales reps actually schedule all of their appointments ahead of time.

Most real estate and insurance agents operate in a similar fashion. Although fuel costs have declined over the past year, this is a very efficient, highly cost-effective method of prospecting and filling a schedule full of appointments with qualified prospects.

While slightly outside the scope of this book, in today's world there are several effective methods of securing a meeting with a potential customer, including email and social media. While those methods can be effective, especially for hard-to-reach, high-value decision makers, my preferred methods are still either the telephone or face-to-face.

Regarding the timeliness of response, people respond to email and social media when it's convenient for them, and typically, that doesn't fill a sales person's schedule quickly enough to grow a business efficiently.

There are still some industries where prospecting is most effectively done face-to-face, the "old school" way. If this is the case, make sure you block an appropriate amount of time into your weekly schedule for prospecting visits.

Some sales organizations label these appointments as "fact finding visits," where the goal is to secure an appointment with the decision maker and discuss information around his business in the process. During a fact-finding visit, the sales person will want to connect with as many individuals within the organization as possible, asking lots of questions.

While in-person visits can take more time to conduct, they are by far the most effective. When it comes down to it, no medium in sales has a greater impact and influence on a customer than looking them squarely in the eye, shaking their hand, and having a real-life conversation.

Have a prospect that's tough to get ahold of by telephone? Why not try stopping in his place of work? Let him know you were in the area, and see if he has a quick minute to talk. The worst he can do is say no.

#5 – Appointments with Prospects

At this point in solidifying a weekly schedule, appointments with prospects need to be entered. Let me clarify, these are purely prospects that should be entered at this point and not current customers!

Typically, the trust and familiarity are not entirely built with prospects at this point in the sales cycle. Therefore, they will be more likely to want you, the sales person, to arrange your schedule around theirs. By entering those appointments at this point in the scheduling process, you will have more flexibility in your schedule to accommodate the high-value targets.

Sales is a numbers game, and in it there's a theory called the "Law of Averages," or as sales veterans refer to it, "LOA." Essentially, LOA is one of the single most empowering philosophies in all of sales. The principle behind it is simple.

If you partake in the same activity for an extended period of time, particularly long enough where an adequate sample size can be collected, you develop averages. Those averages are a direct reflection of your results, based on your skill, customer base, market conditions, and several other factors.

In my years selling CUTCO, we relied on LOA religiously when forecasting for the next year. The three averages that are most important to that business are closing percentage, average order, and phone calls made per appointment scheduled.

When looking at these results, it is also important to break down the numbers based on results with new prospects who do not own the product, and also existing customers who do own it.

Once you know your averages, you can take your

goal for the year, break it down to a specific number of appointments, and then break that total number of appointments into appointments per month, or even per week. Furthermore, that number can even be broken down to the activity needed (phone calls, social media, email, fact-finding visits, etc.) to schedule those appointments.

An important note to remember regarding the Law of Averages is that the sample size has to be large enough to be significant. My recommendation is for a sales person to make at least 100 appointments with qualified prospects before they start to compute their averages.

Also, the Law of Averages is really meant to play out over a long period of time, usually a year. It's too small of a sample size to look at your sales results for just one week. In that situation, outliers carry a much larger weight.

Therefore, the numbers from week to week, and even month to month can be thrown off. However, the Law of Averages generally plays out with a high level of accuracy over the course of a year.

It's important to note that sometimes a prospect will want you to meet with him or her during a period of time you already have blocked out, either for time off, for prospecting calls, or even an appointment with a different prospect or customer. When this happens, it will be very tempting to re-arrange your whole schedule for a big prospect. I know, because I've been there before.

You have a family barbecue scheduled to celebrate Grandma's 80th Birthday, and Paul with ACME Plumbing wants you to meet with him on Sunday night at 6 p.m., because that's the only time he is willing to make time in *his* schedule.

This puts you in a tough position. You've worked so hard to research this guy's company, you've made two trips into his office to uncover valuable information about his business, and you've got the perfect presentation ready for him. You know if he decided to buy from you, it would change your whole year.

At the same time, you know your family will kill you if you miss Grandma's Birthday. Also, at 80 years old, how many more birthdays will Grandma have?

Here's my recommendation. Explain to the prospect that unfortunately, you have an appointment already scheduled for that day, and even tell him specifically what that appointment is. Then, ask him if he will accommodate a different time. If he's a customer you want to work with, he will accommodate and find a different time. If he won't, then either he's not someone you want to align yourself with, or most likely, <u>he doesn't see the value in your product or service, yet</u>. Key word: *yet*.

You cannot allow clients or customers to run your life. There have to be boundaries. It is imperative to the value of your relationships with yourself, your friends, and your family, that you stay true to your schedule.

No matter what.

#6 – Appointments with Existing Customers

In many industries, customers will buy products that need to be serviced over time. Service calls are a great opportunity to reinforce the value of the company, its employees, and the products in the eyes of your customers. These opportunities make the customers feel even better about their decision to purchase a product and work with you.

Examples of great opportunities for service calls are the heating and air conditioning company that, after selling a whole-house unit to a family, offers a free service check-up every year. Another example is a roofing company that offers a free roof check every two years after a purchase of a new roof.

One of the reasons people spend so much money buying CUTCO kitchen knives is because the products come with a forever guarantee. The company guarantees that if any of its products ever break or don't perform as they did when they were purchased, they will be replaced, free of charge. The sales reps of the company take this a step further, offering a free in-home sharpening service any time a customer requests one. Often times, these service calls lead to a customer purchasing more products, and also referring more prospects to the reps. Everyone wins in these appointments.

Regardless of what you're selling, develop some type of service call program. Even if it's just to pop in and see how things are going with their purchase and to re-connect with your customer, do it. The customers will appreciate it and, even if you're in a business where there aren't significant upselling opportunities, your best referrals will always come from your existing customer base.

Imagine your top customer calling her best friend, with you sitting there in her home, and going on and on about how buying your vacuum cleaner was the best purchase she's ever made, and that her friend is crazy if she doesn't invite you over to take a look. As

Jeffrey Gitomer says, "Your present customers are your most underused resource."

You may be asking, "If my present customers are my most underused resource, why are they the #6 thing I put on my calendar each week?" Great question, and really there are a couple of reasons why.

First, your existing customers will be much more flexible with you when it comes to their schedule. Or, if you're popping in unannounced, you minimize the risk of spending a whole day popping in on people who might not be there.

They already like you (hopefully), like the product, and know what they're getting into. With that lower level of apprehension, they will most often be more flexible in allowing you to squeeze them into your schedule, not the other way around.

Secondly, in many industries, the average sale per appointment is much less in a service call than when the customer places his or her initial purchase. While they're extremely valuable, especially for upselling and referral purposes, if most businesses were to schedule the majority of their appointments with service calls only, they would sell a significantly smaller amount than businesses that spent, say, two-thirds of their time with prospects who don't already use the product.

Don't fall into the trap of having too many of your appointments become service calls!

This is a rabbit hole that both new and veteran sales reps will often fall into because existing customers are always more accommodating and nicer. For the sake of your own business, make sure a majority of your time is spent hunting for new business. Push your business forward!

Using your Law of Averages, take your yearly sales goal, and break it down into a monthly goal. From there, you can track your averages for your prospecting appointments and your service appointments. Based on your goals, figure out how many appointments of each per week you will need to do to accomplish those goals.

Then, get on the phone, or get out and schedule the appointments.

#7 – Everything Else

Okay, now that you have your sales schedule handled for the week, this is where you can put in anything else. All of your to-do lists for around the house, groceries, the car wash, picking up your dry cleaning, taking the dog to the groomers, etc. all goes in your schedule now.

If you're filling in your schedule for next week as you're reading this, you'll find something very surprising: you still have a ton of blank, open space in your calendar! All of this is additional free time to do whatever you like.

When you create your schedule in this format, another interesting thing you'll notice is you won't get everything on your to-do list done. And that's okay. Over the years, I've realized that several things I used to put on my to-do list don't need to be completed at all. And if they do really need to be done, they don't necessarily need to be done by me!

Unless you have aspirations of being an expert gardener or are one of those people who has the quintessential "green thumb," I recommend outsourcing your gardening work if you live in a house. If you live in an apartment or condo, please disregard this point. Depending on the size of your house and your personal situation, for many people it also makes sense to hire a housecleaner.

Another option for accomplishing these other items is to hire an assistant. I tend to be cheap, at least that's what my friends say, so I don't do this. Usually, I squeeze these items in either after my sales activities are done for the day, on the weekends, or if I'm driving right by one of these places on the way to a sales appointment. For example, I have to drive right past my dry cleaner almost every time I leave my house, so it's not a big deal for me to take a 45-second detour to drop off or pick up some clothes.

Do whatever works best for you. Remember, though, in sales, you set your own hourly rate. No one sets it for you or determines what you're worth. Be mindful of this fact and realize the time you spend advancing your sales increases your income, while any activity that doesn't advance your sales pulls your income down.

In terms of planning, that's it. As you can see, it doesn't need to be a complicated process. The most important thing is to create a plan that you can stick to. But remember, if you don't execute your plan, you will not see the results.

When you look at any selling industry, across the board, the top sales people share this trait in common. They understand who they need to see and when they are going to see them. Nothing throws them off course.

The underperforming sales people either have no plan, or they create a decent plan and don't have the discipline to stick to it. Thus, they never achieve greatness.

What type of salesperson do you want to be? The choice is yours. I know you will be the type that builds a great plan and works it to the top!

"White space on your
calendar is the enemy of
production and plants the
seeds of doubt."
~ Grant Cardone

ACCESS

"If you leave your card and information about your product, he'll call you if he's interested in meeting," said Sara at the front desk. "Okay, sure," I said, as I tried not to let my frustration with Sara show on my face. So, I left my card, with a leave-behind I had with me, and a personal note asking Pat to call me when he got a moment.

About three hours later my phone rang; it was a number I didn't recognize.

"Hey Bret," the caller said. "This is Pat. What's happening? I didn't even know you stopped by. Why didn't you tell Sara to come get me?"

"Well, she said you were busy in a meeting, and I didn't want to bother you," I replied. "I figured you'd just call me when it was a better time."

"Oh, that girl. Good god, she takes her job too seriously," Pat went on. "Last week my own mother called to talk to me, and she wouldn't even let her through. Don't take it personally. What are you doing later? Let's grab a beer and talk about getting your stuff in here."

After Pat and I locked down the details of the meet-up, I hung up the telephone in shock. I just realized I made one of the biggest mistakes a sales person could make, and unless I had that interaction with Pat, I would have continued to make that same mistake for a lot longer.

That receptionist at the front desk making ten bucks an hour holds a lot of weight. And 99 percent of the time, she has absolutely no clue what you're there for. Her job is to manage her boss' schedule. If she doesn't know who you are, why it's important to let you talk to her boss or decision makers in her company, or decides she doesn't like you, she can kill a whole deal.

Access to the decision maker is everything.

In sales, someone, or a group of people, have to say, "Yes, we want to move forward with your product." Before you even sit down with a prospect to present your product or service, it is essential to know and confirm exactly who will be making the final decision.

You'll know you've missed the mark if you hear:

"Sounds great. Leave the proposal and I'll make sure the boss gets it."

"Let me talk to my business partner. He's going to love this."

"The committee meets next Tuesday. Let me share it with them and I'll get back to you."

"Let me talk to my husband. I always let him make the final call on the decisions involving big money."

Let me put it to you this way. All of these responses are HORRIBLE!

My first years selling in B2B, I used to leave those meetings doing flips over the moon. I knew it was

July, and I might not hit my sales number this month, but September was going to be awesome! Then September happened, and that pipeline of sales coming to fruition revealed itself for what it really was: a pipeline of polite blow-offs and unfulfilled promises.

Finally, I learned what the real problem was. It was me and how I was approaching prospects. I didn't have the correct decision maker, and most of the time I wasn't reaching all of the decision-makers who needed to be included in the sale.

The bottom line here is that access to the decision maker is everything. Some sales trainers say if you don't have access to the decision maker, you are left competing on price alone. I say that's giving the sales person too much credit. If you don't have access to the correct decision makers, you aren't even in the conversation.

In today's monstrously connected society, there's no excuse to not reach the decision maker. There are far too many ways to connect. With telephones, personal networks, social media, and the Internet, there is simply no excuse to call on the wrong person. The only reason you can't reach someone is if you quit trying.

If you want to reach someone, you can - 100% of the time.

Here are some strategies for ensuring you <u>always</u> reach the right person, or people, making the final decision:

#1 - Do your homework

Before you even walk through the door, you

should know who the actual decision maker is. Is there one decision maker who can make the final call? Or are there others who will need to weigh in? Is there a committee that makes these types of decisions? If so, when do they meet?

These questions should all be answered before that receptionist has a chance to turn you away and cost you a sale.

A rabbit hole that sales people often fall into is getting the decision maker right but asking the wrong questions. They might not do the right amount of homework to determine who else has the person's ear. Many times, his wife or partner is a silent decision maker. Right, wrong, or indifferent, most of the time the business owner will not tell you his wife also plays a role in the decision making process.

Never underestimate the influence someone's spouse has on him or her. My wife is a really sharp lady, and often times I'll run tough decisions by her. Her feedback holds a ton of weight in my mind.

About two years ago, I almost fell into this trap. I had a fairly well respected physician in my region who was very interested in purchasing a piece of capital equipment from our company. I had been working with him for several years and had what I considered a pretty solid relationship with him. After discussing the product with him for several months, he approached me in his office one day and asked if I could do a demo for him and his staff. His exact words were, "We're ready to get started with this."

Not thinking anything of it, I scheduled the lunch meeting to bring the product in with one of our product specialists and do an entire presentation for him and his staff. As I was walking out the door, the reception called me back and said, "Oh shoot, Bret. I'm sorry, but we need to pick a different day. Doctor's wife always likes to come to these things. Even though she doesn't practice medicine, she does have an interest in the practice, and especially the money that is spent. You know?"

Ahem. Well, no. I didn't know.

In fact, if the nice lady at the front desk had let me set that appointment without all the pertinent parties present at the demo for the clinical and the financial discussion, it most likely would not have resulted in the sale that I landed after the successful demo.

The funny thing is, the doctor never had any intention in saying his wife weighed in on those types of decisions. Call it ego, machismo, or forgetfulness. The lesson is that you never want to assume anything. Even if you're pretty sure you have all the decision makers included, there's nothing wrong with asking, "Is there anyone else involved in the practice that we should invite to the meeting?"

Aside from a spouse or family member, often times there are business partners or investors who are active in the day-to-day management of the business. If you ask the right questions, you will be sure not to overlook anyone who will contribute to the final decision.

High-level sales trainer Grant Cardone teaches his students to present to the CEO, CFO, and COO in an organization. By doing this, you will get feedback from three different viewpoints, and each person will also give you different information about the company. With additional information, you will be more equipped to expose the need your product or service is going to fill for them.

So how do you find out who the decision makers are? You'll either have to do your homework, ask lower level employees inside the business, or even better, you'll ask the owner of the company directly.

#2 – Have a Gatekeeper "Approach"

The reason most sales people can't get past the gatekeeper comes down to several factors. However, they usually all have two things in common: they come in not knowing what to say, and they don't befriend the gatekeeper. This is what it looks like:

Joe Cool knows he needs to meet with Dave, the Managing Partner of Acme Widgets. So he walks in, and at the front desk sits Daniella, Dave's 22-year-old niece who is home for summer break from college, where she attends San Diego State. Joe Cool walks into Dave's office and, when met by Daniella at the front desk, he has nothing better to say than, "Uhhhh, Hi. Is Dave in today? I was hoping to grab him for a quick minute."

Daniella replies, "Sure, let me see if he's available. Who can I tell him is here?"

"Uh, Joe with Acme Widgets."

"Okay, I'll be right back," responds Daniella, now sniffing out that Joe is a salesman showing up without an appointment and attempting to highjack her uncle's time this morning.

After about two minutes, Daniella comes back, most likely not even discussing the salesman out front with her uncle and says, "I'm sorry, he's in a meeting right now and can't come out. Can you leave your information and he'll call you?"

"Uh, sure. Here's my info. Do you know when a

better time to catch him would be?" pleads Joe.

"Well, he's usually really busy, so the best thing to do is to wait until he calls to schedule an appointment. I'll be sure to give him your information though."

"Okay, great. Thanks for your help today." And Joe leaves.

Help is not what Daniella just offered. What actually happened is she probably went to the break room, brewed herself a fresh cup of hot tea, and didn't actually tell anyone that a time-sucking sales person was out front.

By the end of the summer, after repeating that event no less than 100 times, Daniella earned a PhD in Professional Gatekeeping for Business from her Uncle Dave's company. For those keeping score at home, thousands of these degrees are given out around the world. Daily.

Here are a few tips to more effectively work WITH the gatekeeper to get the appointment with the decision maker(s):

1. <u>Build rapport and make friends</u> – Like it or not, the girl (or guy) at the front holds a lot of power, especially if you haven't gotten the business as a customer yet. Introduce yourself, get to know her, ask where she's from, how long she's worked there, how she came to work for the business, etc. Don't be afraid to get to know her, ask about her aspirations within the company, or tell a funny story. The key: loosen up and have fun!

2. <u>Ask for help</u> – People, especially women, love to help others. Sometimes, simply saying, "Daniella, I need your help with something

I'm working on," can be enough to get the gatekeeper's attention, and may push them just far enough to help get you that appointment.

3. Educate them on the value of meeting – Having a solid, crisp, 15-second description of why it is crucial you meet with her boss sets you apart from every other bumbling, unprepared salesperson she will encounter. Imagine saying this: "Hi, Daniella. How are you today? I'm hoping you can help me. I know your uncle is really busy, and my widgets could help him increase the business' productivity and profitability by a significant amount of money this year. Have you seen these widgets before?" (Give her a brief, 60-second explanation of the product and the need it fills.) "If you could help me get a short appointment with him, I'm sure he will be able to see what I'm saying. If we meet and he disagrees, that's fine too. I just need the opportunity to chat with him for a few minutes. When would be a good time to catch him for a few minutes?"

4. Follow Up – Send her an email, or even better, a handwritten card thanking her for her help. I guarantee you'll be the only sales person she gets a personally written card from. From the rest, she will just get attitude after she screens them out.

Lackluster salespeople approach the gatekeeper with the completely wrong outlook and strategy, and it shows. Instead of looking at the gatekeeper as your adversary and trying to beat them down and punch them in the mouth to get to their boss, how about trying to align yourself with them? Focus on showing them that you understand and value the position they hold within the company. Respect them as a person, and try to make friends with them. Try it. It works!

If you've tried getting past the gatekeeper multiple times, and you still aren't getting anywhere, then it's time to try a different approach.

#3 – Get Creative

"Busy morning already, yeah?" questioned Jake as he walked up to the loading dock at 6:50 a.m. For a rainy, blustery day in northern California, the receiving workers had been hard at work for nearly three hours.

"Yeah, no doubt. It's amazing how many shipments we get in on Monday morning," replied one of the workers.

Because one of the workers was struggling to lift a couch off the truck, Jake dropped his planner and offered to lend him a hand, which the worker graciously accepted.

After about five minutes of small talk, Jake said to the one of the workers, "Hey, do you guys know where I could find Ron, the owner? I was trying to catch him this morning before he gets going."

Instantly, one of the workers leads Jake right back to Ron's office, where the owner is reading the morning paper, drinking a cup of coffee.

"Excuse me, sir," said the worker. "This young man who just helped me unload a shipment would like to catch you for a minute before you get going."

"Oh, sure thing," replied Ron. "Come on in. What can I do for you this morning?"

And just like that, Jake is sitting in the owner's office, ready to engage him in a conversation regarding how he can help his company be more successful.

The saying "think outside the box" has been the most overused cliché in business over the past two decades, and for good reason. To reframe it, what it really means is, "Don't think and act like everyone else," and "if what you're doing isn't working, try something else."

Have you ever been out to a social gathering, struck up a conversation with a complete stranger, and ended up becoming friends with that person? Whether it's another parent or teacher at your kids' Back-to-School night, another parent at your kids' soccer game, or a nice old man at the grocery store, you have the ability to be likeable and for your presence and attention to be well-received by others.

So, if the word "salesman" isn't stapled across your forehead and the stigma of an annoying salesperson isn't tacked on your tail by the receptionist, then the barriers preventing you from accessing the decision maker are gone.

How do you do that? Especially if you're having no luck going through the front door of a business? You get creative and take a different approach. In most businesses, there's another way in.

Jake is a top rep on my sales team, and the example just used was a story he told me during our initial interview to work for my company. When hiring people for sales positions, I want them to demonstrate to me they have the ability to get to the decision makers, even if the more conventional method has been challenged.

The example he gave me was exactly what I was looking for. It demonstrated an ability to be creative and get to a decision maker. Moreover, it showed me Jake has a can-do attitude and will do whatever it takes to get in front of the decision maker. Obviously, he got the job and is doing quite well for himself.

Here are some of the best non-conventional approaches to gaining access to a decision maker:

1. <u>Find someone in the trenches</u> – Similar to Jake's example, find a way to approach one of the employees of the business who is not the receptionist. People who don't work the front desk are not professional gatekeepers. Better yet, find a sales person within the company. Sales people want to talk to everyone, and they usually want to be helpful. If you can get a sales person talking to you, he'll frequently take you right to the owner or CEO.

2. <u>Mutual friends or contacts</u> – Is there anyone in your network that your prospect is particularly close with? If you can get a personal introduction and endorsement (also known as a testimonial), that can be the easiest way in.

3. <u>Social media / email</u> – There are several strategies and tactics for connecting with a customer or prospect via the digital world. This is a huge complex issue, and entire books have been written on effectively utilizing social media to drive sales results. To keep it brief here, often times "friending" prospects, liking a few of their posts, and looking for a way to provide value or information can be enough to get them to know you well enough to agree to an appointment. Just make sure to not seem

pesky or annoying, and avoid looking like you're contacting them with a "hidden agenda." That will surely backfire 100% of the time.

4. <u>Charitable/Community events</u> – When I was in more traditional business-to-business sales, I joined a local Rotary Club and also a business networking group call LeTip. While different in nature, my time with both organizations was extremely beneficial. I had the opportunity to give back to the community and meet other business owners who are still friends today. I also benefited business-wise from my time in those groups. Here's a tip. To gain the full benefit of membership, you must go into the group looking to give with no ulterior motive. It is when people see that you are truly a giver that the true opportunities start to be unlocked. Get involved, work toward a board position, and participate in the events. It's more enjoyable and fulfilling, and you'll also be known in your community as a mover-and-shaker.

Finally, here are a few books I highly recommend on gaining access to decision makers, and creating mutually beneficial relationships with these contacts:

1. *The Power to Get In* – by Michael Boylan
2. *Cold Calling Techniques (That Really Work!)* – by Stephan Schiffman
3. *Givers Gain: The BNI Story* – by Ivan Misner, PhD
4. *Networking Like a Pro: Turning Contacts into Connections* – by Ivan Misner, PhD
5. *The Tao of Twitter: Changing Your Life and Business*

140 Characters at a Time – by Mark Schaefer

"You can get everything in life you want if you help enough other people get what they want."
~ Zig Ziglar

SELLING SKILLS

Going back to that day of field training with Adam Curchack, I learned there was a lot that I didn't know about selling. There were specific practices and habits that, at the time, I had not yet built into my own repertoire. The other glaring thing that stood out: I needed to learn how to sell.

My selling skills sucked.

Regarding selling skills, the key takeaway, or idea I gathered was "engagement." Adam knew how to engage his customers. Before we arrived at his appointments that day, none of those customers woke up and said, "Honey, let's drop 800 bucks on knives today, and then write down 10 of our friends for this guy to see."

They knew a guy was coming over to show them some knives that their crazy friends had bought, thinking they'd do their friends a solid and let the guy come over. But they certainly weren't *buying* any of the knives. On top of that, they weren't going to sick some sales leach onto their friends. *They don't do that.*

What does that even mean? They don't "do that"?

What is *that*?

After spending the day with Adam, I realized I needed to step up my habits, and also my selling skills. I knew if I didn't get better, I wasn't going to reach the level of success I was looking for.

The sales process is an intrinsic process with several moving pieces. Entire books have been written, and training seminars exist, on several of the individual aspects of the selling process and the skills encompassing it. Several of those skills will be discussed in more detail in this chapter.

However, there's one brutal truth you can't get away from, especially when discussing building better selling skills: Experience matters. You have to apply the skills in real selling situations with a great amount of repetition before measurable improvements can be made.

You can read all the sales books, watch all the YouTube videos, and even attend sales seminars. And you should do all of those things. However, the best way to improve your skills is to implement the skills immediately, and then practice them over and over again.

In the pharmaceutical and medical device industry, when we train sales people on new products and new ways of selling existing products, we have them role-play with one another in the training session. This allows them to take the new information, implement it immediately, and start to hone their talk tracks, so when they're in front of their customer, the message comes out more organically.

In sales, some appointments go well, and some completely flop. And that's okay. Every time you practice your presentation aloud, you will improve.

Every time you practice them in front of a customer, you will improve even more. Over time, after hundreds and hundreds of appointments, your skills will be very solid.

That's what happened to me.

Going back to my day with Adam, I realized three keys things:

1. I had it in me to be one of the best salespeople in my industry.
2. I wasn't doing enough appointments, even at my current skill level, to achieve my goals.
3. If I did more appointments, my skills would improve dramatically, and I'd achieve even greater results.

In the coming months, and the years following, all three of those assumptions proved to be true. As you develop your skill level, here are some specific selling skills you will want to master on your way to becoming one of the best in your industry.

Prospecting

We discussed the importance of reaching the decision makers in the previous chapter. Before that point comes prospecting and qualifying, which is the process where you identify who those decision makers are, and if they're even a good fit for your product or service.

If you want to increase your results in appointments, the first thing you need to look at is which customers you are spending your time in front of. One of the reasons salespeople underperform is because they spend their time in front of people who really aren't qualified to buy what they're selling. In the medical device industry, physicians who do not do surgery are very interested in learning about the surgical products that are being used. One of the reasons they're so interested is because the experienced sales people, who know those people couldn't use their products even if they wanted to, don't ever call on them. But then a new rep comes along who doesn't know any better.

The physician will want to hear everything about the new product lines. He'll have his whole office staff attend the lunch. Heck, he'll even invite a bunch of med school students from the teaching institution down the street. You'll spend $200 of your company's money showing this doctor, and 15 other people who can't use the products, all your stuff.

At the end of the day, asking the question, "Doctor Smith, how many days a week do you operate?" would have solved a lot of problems. When the answer, "Oh, I don't operate anymore. I leave that to the younger guys getting all the new, improved training I never got," would have saved the company $200, and most importantly, allowed the sales person to spend her time in front of physicians who actually can use her products.

Regardless of what industry you're selling in, you have to know who your target market is. It really comes down to three basic questions:

1. Who has a need for my product?
2. Can they afford to buy it? (If not now, in the future is fine.)
3. Can they refer me to others who can also benefit from and afford my product or service?

If you're a real estate agent, do you want to spend

all of your time marketing homes to college students with no income or to people with horrible credit who can't get a loan? What about people who just bought their house a year ago? They could be interested in purchasing a vacation or investment property, or maybe they know someone who might be in the market for a home.

Or maybe that nice newly-wed couple who scraped all their pennies together to get pre-approved for the $200,000 home, ropes you into driving them around to 16 different houses on a Sunday, only to tell you at the end, "It's a lot of money. We just need to think about it."

If you're going to invest all that time and effort, why wouldn't you try to spend more of your time with the client that can afford a $400,000 or $500,000 home? Obviously, you would. I also realize market conditions, and the availability of buyers at different income levels factors into the equation as well.

But how do you get more $500,000 buyers and less $200,000 looky-loos? You target them and spend more of your time promoting to them.

At CUTCO, they teach the new sales reps to target people who are married, working, and own their own home. If they have kids and are the type to host the Little League barbecues, that's always a plus.

When you stop and think about it, if you're selling high-end kitchen products, the people who are most likely to INVEST in those items are exactly those people. They've invested in a home, so they are already in the mindset of investing in nice things for their home.

If they own a home and entertain to some degree, they will want nice things that make that experience more enjoyable. Also, if they work, they will be more likely to have the money to spend on products like that.

A fantastic way to find more qualified prospects is to approach your current and past customers for referrals. Past customers who've had a positive experience with you and the product or service you offer are your best assets as a sales person. They're walking testimonials. So let them open the door for you to others.

Approach your current customers and ask them how things are going for them. Let them know you are doing a free giveaway, special discount, contest, or anything else cool you can think of, for the customer who can refer you to the most friends. Or, if the profit margin works for you to do this, look at giving something free every time an existing customer refers a client your way! Even a $10 Starbucks gift card works.

During my days selling CUTCO, if a customer wrote down ten referrals for me, I'd throw in a free vegetable peeler, pizza cutter, or ice cream scoop with their order. If they didn't buy anything, and they wrote down a bunch of contacts they thought would be great prospects for me anyways, I'd go out to my car and get them a small utility knife before I left. Many times, those people would call me back in the future and would be in a better position to buy.

Regardless, just because someone doesn't perceive himself to be a good fit for your product or service doesn't mean he doesn't know people who might be.

During the holiday season of 2004, I did a presentation for a young couple who was extremely interested in buying from me. However, they were just starting out, had just bought their first house, had three young children under five years old, and the holidays were fast approaching. At the end of the appointment, Jennifer said to me, "Bret, I'd love to buy these, and I'd use them a ton. We just can't afford it right now.

"But...I do want to send you to my Mom. She's a big cook and would probably buy the whole set from you." Well, her mother, Robin, did buy the whole set from me. Along with it, she also bought four additional sets for Jennifer and her three siblings' families as well.

Find the Problem – Expose the Need

Before any product or service is sold, there must be a need, or a perceived void, that it fills. Notice I say "perceived" need or void. People don't buy what they need. They buy what they want and then attempt to justify their purchase with the logic that they just filled a need they perceive to have.

Or better yet...they filled a void that a good sales person showed them they had.

To illustrate this fact, look at the sales of iPhones, clothing, jewelry, automobiles, and the most common one, Starbucks. Do people really "need" this stuff to survive? Of course not.

However, we've been conditioned by great sales and marketing efforts to believe we do. And that, ladies and gentlemen, is the art of sales.

Most of what people buy is not essential to living, staying warm, and safe. At least not in the quantity and quality that we consume. Although we trick ourselves into thinking we need things, the reality is that they add value to our lives. They make life more enjoyable.

Regardless of what you're selling, your product or service must fill a specific need. In most cases, the customer won't even know that need exists, at least before you show up. When you work for a sales organization, this need will be well clarified, and you will be trained on that exact need. If you are in business for yourself, you will need to build this into your presentation.

Once you've properly conveyed the need, you can:

Offer the Solution

Once the customer acknowledges (and not always verbally) there's a need or a void you've helped her uncover, the next step in the selling process is to offer your solution to that problem. If this part of the selling process isn't done properly, you will not set yourself up to close the deal.

This is where the true interest and the desire to buy are built. It's also called "building value." An entire book could be devoted to this topic and is definitely a possibility later on in this book series. For now, here are four quick tips to offering the solution, creating interest, and building the prospect's desire to "want" what you're selling.

Features and benefits – This can get complicated, so I'll simplify it for you. What are three or four key features about your product that make it worth buying? If you sell a product that has more than this number of items that make it fantastic, great! However, that's too much, and you'll lose the customer after the 4th one anyway.

So, what are the top features or characteristics that make the product exceptional AND that put it ahead of its competition? Those are the features you want to focus on.

The first time I spoke on the same program as Hal Elrod, he gave a presentation to a bunch of new reps that I've still never forgotten. In the presentation, he said, "The features are what the product does. The real value of the product is in the *benefits*."

To summarize, take the three or four unique aspects of your product, and then tell how and why they are beneficial to the customer. For example, CUTCO knives come with a handle made out of a material called celcon, and the blade of the knife is made out of surgical grade, high carbon stainless steel. What that means for the customer is, the knife handle won't melt in the dishwasher, and the blade holds a sharp edge for a long time, while not rusting in the dishwasher.

"So it's dishwasher safe," reiterated Hal.

If you're a plumber, you know all too well that a high percentage of calls don't come in during the "normal business hours" of 8 a.m. to 5 p.m. So being available 24 hours a day and carrying 354 different pieces of piping and fittings are probably features you've used to build your business.

However, that doesn't mean anything to a customer until you tell them, "I'm available whenever you have a problem, even in the middle of the night, and when I come out, I generally have everything needed to fix your plumbing issue right then and there. I'll make sure your needs get taken care of."

Get it? I think you do.

Third-party stories / testimonials -- David H. Comins once said, "People will accept your ideas much more readily if you tell them Benjamin Franklin said it first." I stole that quote from an article I read several years ago from the great sales trainer Bob Burg (I highly recommend you also read his work).

While this statement does contain some humor, it really sums up what we are trying to do as salespeople, which is trying to get our customers and prospects to respect our ideas as they would someone they trust completely. Since no one alive actually knew Ben Franklin, that's not an option.

However, there are people your prospects and customers know and respect, who are enjoying the benefits of owning your product or service. Those stories have to be told during your presentation of the solution.

Three weeks ago I listed a property to sell, and I had my landscaper at the property to assess what work needed to be done to sell the house. After he had given me the three different options that he and his crew could do to spruce the property up, I asked him, "Well you do this every day. If price didn't matter, what would get this place sold the fastest, and how much is too much to spend on the yard?" I wanted validation from other clients.

What if you don't have the relationship with your customer that my landscaper and I have, where I trust his expert opinion? You have to build that, and the best way is through telling stories during your presentation about real people, just like them, thinking the same things they are thinking now as they ponder whether or not to buy from you.

They should be stories about people who

ultimately decided to buy and who are very happy with their decision. If those stories and testimonials can be from other people they know and respect, or at least people they've heard of, even better.

One final thought on testimonials and third-party stories: If you're going to use a third-party story in a sales situation, make sure the prospect doesn't dislike the person serving as the example. For example, Donald Trump would not be the best person to use as a third-party endorsement for your product or service.

Even if The Donald has used your widgets for years and years, he is not only a controversial figure, but also a very visible political figure these days. Whether you love him or hate him is inconsequential. The reality is, there will be a certain percentage of your audience that doesn't connect with your message, especially if they disagree with his political stance.

Business is tough enough to get. Why would you want to piss off even a percentage of your audience? Do and say things that connect with your customers. Don't do things that will disconnect.

Mini-closes -- Mini-closes are a very effective tool to use throughout a sales appointment. An example could be, after explaining how your company offers a lifetime guarantee, asking the prospect, "So, Mrs. Jones, can you see why we've been in business so long?" Or even better, "John, can you see why all your friends bought this stuff?"

If you're selling a house to a client, you could say "So Mr. and Mrs. Stevens, you stated you wanted a big, open floor plan so you can entertain. Do you like that about this house?"

Essentially, mini-closes, also called trial closes, serve a couple of purposes. First, they are a great way to test how well your prospect is receiving and buying into your message and service offering. Secondly, studies show when a person gets in the habit of saying "Yes" throughout an appointment, it reduces the chance of getting a "No" at the end when you ask for the sale.

Most importantly, they're a great way to tailor the product or service to the customer, and to show the prospect that you are listening and working to accommodate their wants and needs. So, what if a customer says "no" during a trial close?

That's okay, because it gives you an opportunity to clarify exactly what they're looking for. If you know they're not satisfied yet then it gives you the opportunity to either find an option that better suites the client, or advise the client that you can't meet their expectations so you both can move on.

Close the Sale

Much has been written over the years on the best "closing" techniques. There are definitely best practices for getting that final commitment from the prospect to move forward, and I'll discuss a few strategies and tactics here. With that in mind, at this point in the appointment, the sale should already be made. Both the sales person and the prospect should already know if the prospect is buying.

If you get to the end of a presentation, ask for the order, and are surprised when the customer says no, you did something wrong throughout the presentation. I remember back several years ago when my wife and I were dating, and things were starting to get more serious.

After being friends for over 15 years *before* we started dating, and then dating for several months, I knew she was the one I wanted to spend the rest of my life with. We were starting to talk a lot about our future together, and things were going well. One evening after dinner, we walked by a jewelry store, and one particular ring caught my wife's eye. She made a comment about how nice it would be to get a ring like that. Being the devil's advocate I can sometimes be, I asked, "Yeah, that ring is stunning. But what if I propose to you and you say no?"

Without skipping a beat, she looked back at me and said, "You don't ask the question until you know what the answer is going to be."

The final close is the same way. Whether or not a customer is buying should never be the question. The only questions should be what are they buying, how much, when do they want delivery, and what are the necessary payment arrangements that work best for that prospect? That's it.

I remember watching the movie *Boiler Room*, where Ben Affleck says in his famous scene in front of all the new hires, "Always be closing." Truer words about sales have never been spoken. However, people confuse what those words really mean.

When people hear the phrase "Always be closing," I think they get a perception of a salesman in a suit, with over-gelled, slicked back hair, glad-handing, and spending every minute of every interaction telling his prospects why they need to buy what he's selling. While that may have been what they were trying to portray in that movie, that's not what is meant to happen in a real-life selling situation.

Closing is a continuous process that should happen from the moment you first make contact with a prospect. It should be a comfortable interaction, almost like dining with a friend, so when you get to the end of the presentation, both parties already know whether or not the prospect is moving forward with the purchase.

With that in mind, there does come a point in the presentation where the sales person has to ask for a firm commitment from the prospect. After working with the prospect throughout the entire appointment, you must ask them if they want to place an order today.

On asking for the order, I have three rules every sales person should follow:

1. However you are going to ask for the order, you have to ask.
2. When you ask for the order, add the word today to the end of the question.
3. Once you ask for the order, do not respond until the prospect gives you a definite yes or no. Then count slowly to five in your head before you respond.

There are a million different ways a salesperson can ask a prospect for the order. The reality is, the exact words don't matter. What is important is that you make the question feel as confident and natural as possible.

In keeping it simple, here are a couple of examples:

"So would you like to get started today?"

"Are you good with me putting in your order today?"

"Can I go ahead and help you place your order today?"

"Let's get your order placed today. When would you like delivery?"

Really, that's all it has to be. One of the biggest mistakes I see sales organizations make is, when placing importance on the closing process, they make the final question sound too formal or rehearsed, so it doesn't come across to the customer in a natural and confident manner.

The reason the word "today" is important is that it adds a sense of urgency to the customer, without coming across as a "pushy" sales person. Using the word today reinforces the agreement that the customer will be committing to buying now. By not being specific on the decision being made "today," often times prospects will push you off by asking you to come back next week, month, year, etc.

Most times customers have legitimate concerns as to why they can't move forward in the process. Remember, if you're selling a great product, getting a smaller order of the product in the customer's hands today is better than a promise for a larger order from that prospect in the future. If the customer is using the product, she will feel the value of it in her hands every day. If she's not feeling that value, all the customer will remember is the sticker price.

Most importantly, when you ask the final question to the prospect if he wants to move forward with your product, it's time to shut up and go silent. I'm serious. After you ask the question, "So John, would you like me to get your order placed today?" you zip your lip and don't say anything.

The customer will do one of a few different things. If he's ready to get started, he'll simply say, "Sure, let's get started." If he says that, then stop talking, get out an order form, and start filling out the contract!

If you get anything other than a yes, then that means the customer has some reservations about moving forward with the product. The key is, you have to get the true objection out, and the only way to do that is to let the customer talk. This is where crappy sales people get it wrong.

If the customer doesn't say yes, usually he will say something like, "No, we just can't do it." A bad sales person usually responds at this point, either trying to ask questions, start the B.S. objection cycle they teach you in new hire training, or by trying to re-sell the customer on why he should buy. When this happens, the prospect's walls go up. You're now just another sales person with his or her own agenda. You didn't listen, and in the eyes of that prospect, he's done with you.

You just cut the lifeline.

A better way to approach this situation is by sitting there in silence. The customer will go back and forth, hem and haw over it, and then say, "No, we just can't do it right now." When you get the definite "No," sit there in silence and count to five in your head. (It really works best if it's five full seconds, but I know if I told everyone to wait five seconds there'd be a percentage of people that would faint while trying this).

Silence is uncomfortable in a pressure-filled situation. Have you ever been in a room where people have been somber and silent over something, where everyone was afraid to throw out that icebreaker? Almost invariably, isn't there always someone who tries to cut it, make a joke, or make light of the situation? That person could handle the uncomfortable silence the least.

In sales, you want to be the one who handles silence the best.

After the prospect gives you a definitive "no," sit there in silence. Let him break the uncomfortable silence first. Dan Cassetta, one of the great longtime sales leaders at CUTCO, used to say, "The first one who talks is buying. They're either buying you and your product, or you're buying why they can't get it."

Once your prospect breaks the silence, this is where the true objection comes out. There are only about five or six true objections that will really come out. Here's a list of the most common ones:

"We'd love to move forward with ordering, but we've already blown our budget for the whole year."

"I'd love to buy from you today, but I have to let my business partner weigh in."

"I can't make this large of a decision without discussing it with my husband first."

"This is just too much to spend right now."

"It's great stuff. It's just more than I need."

If you've done your qualifying correctly on the front end, and the prospect has a need for and is able to afford your product, then there are only a few potential reasons for them to object. Either they don't understand the value, the package you're showing them needs to be tailored more specifically to fit their needs, or they can't afford to go with the combination you're showing them. Those are really the only possible objections.

Once you get the true objection out, acknowledge and validate the prospect's concern with moving forward. A solid approach is to say, "John, I completely understand where you're coming from.

Thank you for sharing that with me. Other prospects in your position express the same concern all the time. I think I may have something that might address the concern you just raised. Do you mind if I show you?"

At that point, you can offer a myriad of different options, and far too many to be covered within the scope of this book (although they may be included in another *Selling Edge* book in the near future ☺). However, your best bet is to find out what they're comfortable committing to TODAY. Take the order, get the customer on board, and let him or her increase their usage as their confidence and experience with your product increases over time.

Get Referrals

Most sales companies spend millions upon millions of dollars each year on their marketing budget and spend almost nothing to show appreciation for existing and past customers. It's the most "bass-ackward" way of doing business you could ever imagine.

Why would you spend tons of money going and trying to recruit people who don't know your company or products, don't have any relationship with you, and couldn't tell why they should pick you and not your competitor across town?

Great question, huh? The answer is *you shouldn't*.

Here's a tip: take the money you were going to spend on advertising this year, and re-allocate it to "Customer Appreciation / Referral Program." If you get a customer of yours who had a great experience with you and your product, get her on the phone with

5-10 of her friends; she will do half of the selling for you.

Let's look deeper at the example of CUTCO for a minute and why that business model works so well for the company. They have a bunch of college kids in their early twenties walking into the homes of complete strangers, often times while the husband is at work and the wife and kids are home alone, with a bag full of knives that cut with surgical precision. Really?

I know when I came home from the interview, that's the first thing my parents said.

Yet, after over sixty years in existence, the company has over 200 offices nationally, contracts with roughly 60,000 college students each year, and has continued to grow revenue year over year, regardless of the economic circumstances of the country. In my mind, the three main reasons are: the products are phenomenal, the sales leaders recruit and train new reps extremely well, and the reps promoting them understand how to generate interest and then get an abundance of qualified referrals from customers.

Here are the best tips for getting qualified referrals from customers:

1. Build a solid rapport where your customer will want to help you.
2. Tell your customer at the beginning that you get your customers from referrals of customers just like them.
3. Follow a specific approach.
4. Ask for referrals every time.

For a customer to feel comfortable writing down 10 of their friends on a sheet of paper, or even one or two for that matter, they must feel comfortable and like you enough to ask their friends to spend the same time with you they did. If a prospect or customer says, "I don't do that to my friends," they are really saying that they were happy to help you out, but haven't been made to feel comfortable enough to sick you on all their friends.

The best way to overcome this objection is to work harder on the principles outlined in Chapter 2 on building a great connection with others. If a customer likes you, trusts you, and genuinely enjoyed spending time with you during the appointment, then they should want to help you get in front of more people.

During my day with Adam, we encountered this example during our second appointment. When we arrived, his prospect Mary said to us, "I do need a couple of things, so I'll buy some stuff from you. But I'm not doing that to my friends."

"Okay, that's fine," replied Adam. "How about we make a deal? That's the same thing your friend Sally said at first. After the presentation, she felt comfortable enough with me, and liked the product, and ended up thinking you'd enjoy this as well. Would you be okay holding off that final decision until after the presentation?"

"Sure," shot back Mary with a smile.

After the presentation, and as Adam was writing up Mary's order, she said to him, "So now's probably the point where I have to write down some of my friends, right?"

"If you liked me," said Adam. "Only if you liked me and the presentation. It helps me out a lot. If you can think of a few of your friends, I promise I'll make them feel just as comfortable as you did."

Adam and I walked out the door about ten minutes later, with a signed order for $600 and a list of ten of Mary's friends for Adam to call.

Not being comfortable giving referrals is normal for most people. Although some prospects and customers will write down their friends if you're telling them you have ice to sell to Eskimos, most people are not initially comfortable with the thought of referring someone they don't know to close friends. What if the person is weird? Is this person safe to be around? What if he's a high-pressured sales person? What if you can't get him to leave? What if they wonder if it's even safe to be alone with you?

These are all the thoughts that are going through a prospect's head at first, and it's completely understandable for them to feel this way. Informing the prospect that you will be asking her for referrals at the beginning of the presentation is the best way to break the ice. First, it doesn't make asking for them at the end seem like some huge elephant in the room. Second, it plants the thought in her head ahead of time, so during the conversation, it will help her think of friends that might also have an interest in your product or service.

Following a specific approach, and saying it the same way every single time, is vital. For some reason, new reps always think they need to re-invent the wheel on this one, as if for some reason, they know more about selling a product than a company that's been successful for 65 years, or, in many cases, longer.

Steph Curry is the reigning MVP of the National Basketball Association and is one of the fastest-growing sports stars on the planet. A remarkable basketball player, he is best known for being a lights-out 3-point shooter. If you were taking a shooting lesson from Steph Curry, and he recommended certain fundamentals to practice to make you a better shooter, wouldn't you take his advice? Or would you argue with him and make up a thousand excuses why that wouldn't work for you?

If you're smart, you'd take his advice, try to model it as closely as possible, and practice those fundamentals every day. Sales is no different. High achievers have practices, systems, and habits in place that propelled them to the top of their industry. If you follow those same approaches and hone them over time, you can achieve those results as well.

Even the tenured, top-notch reps have a referral approach that they follow with exact consistency, every single time. It's pretty simple. When it comes to asking for referrals, you must ask in the most concise, genuine, upfront manner, and you must ask with the expectation that all your customers give them to you.

After Mary told Adam that she'd write down a couple names, Adam handed her his referral notebook. As he was flipping to an open page for her to use, Adam had to flip through several pages that were already filled out by customers. Each page he flipped through had no less than ten referrals on it.

"Wow, so if I didn't give you any names, I probably would have been the only one who didn't," Mary remarked.

To that Adam joked, "Well, not the first one ever. But you definitely would have been the first one in a while."

As a sales person, your two most important documents are your customer list and your referral list. Period. They are your lifeline, your pipeline, and your financial livelihood.

The best sales people ask for referrals every single time, without exception. Regardless of whether or not a customer buys from you, networking, gathering referrals, and prospecting is an ongoing process even more important than closing itself. If you want to sell, you must have people to sell to.

A common question people often ask me is, "How do I build my skills and become one of the best?" The answer is "through massive action and learning from experience."

The only way to truly build your selling skills and improve your effectiveness as a sales person is by doing more appointments than anyone else, letting the numbers play out how they will, and then learning from that experience. Mentors can teach you a ton and significantly shorten the learning curve. You can learn fantastic talk tracks and sales techniques from books. You can even design the most organized schedule possible.

At the end of the day, the X-factor that matters most, shortens the learning curve the most, and increases your effectiveness the fastest, is taking massive action. Make as many appointments as you possible can.

After I had returned home from my day with Adam, I realized three key takeaways:

1. My skills were better than I thought they were.
2. I wasn't doing enough appointments to generate the results I wanted.
3. If I scheduled more appointments, my skill set would improve much faster than it was at the

moment.

As I recapped the conversations Adam had with his customers, I remembered several similar conversations I had with my own customers. The words he was saying weren't really any different. What was different was the fluidity of the conversations and the laid back, confident vibe Adam gave off. He was at ease, and it put his customers at ease.

Adam had been selling CUTCO for several years. He was one of the fastest reps ever to reach the company's Hall of Fame. After doing thousands and thousands of presentations with prospects and customers, he had faith in himself and the product, and he knew in his heart that people would buy it. He had experienced this thousands of times over the years, so those four appointments that day weren't a big deal at all. They were just another piece in a huge pie of experience he had to draw from.

I didn't have that level of experience or thousands of examples to draw from, and that's where a lot of my fear came from. With that fear came apprehension. Ultimately, that apprehension was causing me to limit the amount of action I was taking toward my goals.

It was simple. I needed to get on the phone, schedule a ton of appointments, use the new skills and outlook I learned from Adam, Hal, Jesse, and several others, and have faith that the results would follow. Those results did come, and, over time, they escalated to levels I never thought were initially possible. But it all started with getting on the phone, scheduling appointments, and doing as many of them as I possibly could.

As Wayne Gretzky once said, "You will miss 100%

of the shots you don't take."

Take shots. Get in front of customers and do your best. Some appointments will suck, and many times, especially when you're new, *you* will suck. However, many appointments will also go very well. Over time, the number of those great appointments and sales will increase. As long as you learn and improve from your experiences, you will be on your way to becoming one of the best in your industry.

But it all starts with that first appointment. From there, don't look back.

"You will miss 100% of the shots you don't take."
~ Wayne Gretzky

CONCLUSION

Mark Lovas, founder and CEO of the quickly-rising shirt manufacturer Trumaker, is one of the most amazing people I've ever met. I first met Mark in 2001 during my first CUTCO summer conference. During his time as CUTCO'S North Pacific Division Manager, his division was #1 in the company for five consecutive years. Some of the most successful reps and managers in the company's history were personally recruited and trained by Mark. Tall, slender, and possessing a dynamic personality, he commanded the attention of the room like no one else. When you met him, it was easy to see why his team was always at the top of the rankings.

During his keynote message that evening, he said the most accurate statement about sales and life that I've ever heard, even to this day: **It won't be perfect, and it doesn't need to be perfect for you to be successful.**

At the time, I was so new to sales and so inexperienced in life that I didn't fully grasp the meaning of his words. However, in the 15 years since I first heard the statement, it continues to resonate with me, and I continue to see it play out every day.

Sales is a fascinating, challenging, fun business to be in. In many ways, it's a small microcosm of life and how the world works. Your results are a direct reflection of your efforts, or lack thereof. In sales, as in life, things happen that you don't have any control over. However, you do have control over how you respond and what you do about it.

As Epictetus said, "It's not what happens to you, but how you react to it that matters."

You can't control the weather. If a product is on back order, you can't control that either. You can't control what others say about you. For those who have young children, you know you definitely can't control what they think and do.

If traffic is congested, you can't do anything to change that. When someone treats you poorly, they made that choice, not you. A batter in baseball can't control what the pitcher throws. Football offenses can't control if the defense decides to bring the house with the blitz. Ballerinas can't control the other dancers in a recital. A surfer can't control how the waves come into shore.

Most of what happens in life, we have no control over. What we do have absolute control over is how we internalize it, and the action we decide to take in response to it.

Remember the Law of Averages (pronounced "Lowa") discussed earier in this book? We have total control over how we utilize the idea of the LOA. Here's an example of LOA in action. Sara is a sales rep for ACME widgets, and her goal is to sell $1 million worth of widgets this year, which could be a daunting task and might even seem impossible. Or is it? That seems like a lot of widgets to sell, doesn't it?

Until we break down the numbers and quantify how many units that is, and if it's reasonable to expect that number of units, we would have no way of knowing.

Sara has been with ACME for three years full-time in her current role. A consistent above-average performer in the company, last year was her best year, selling just over $800,000 of widgets. The two years prior she sold $762,000 and $757,000. Based on her tenure of three years, and the fact that she's worked full-time in her role for this length of time, we have a large enough sample size to assess her past performance, and then use those numbers to map out the action required by her to top $1 million this year.

If we go back and track the number of appointments she's done over the past three years, there are three key metrics we will need: number of appointments completed, number of sales, and average order size. Another variable that really helps and isn't always possible in all industries, is to also look at the activity that's required to set each appointment.

For example, during my time at CUTCO, we used to block out "phone time" in our calendar. This was our primary method for setting 95% of our appointments. We kept a tally of every phone call we made; after we had completed several hundred appointments, we could look at the number of calls it took to schedule each appointment. Further, we also tracked how many no-shows or cancellations we averaged per month, and would start scheduling that many extra appointments as well. However, all selling industries differ to some extent, and you don't always have direct control over the appointment-setting numbers.

Let's look at how many appointments Sara will need to complete to surpass her goal of $1 million. When breaking down her yearly goal, she will need to sell $83,000 monthly to surpass $1 million for the year. Over the past three years, she completed an average of 429 appointments per year, with 258 of the appointments resulting in orders placed. That average, which is called her "Closing Ratio," is 60%. When you take her total dollars sold, and divide that by the number of sales she closed, that comes to $3,000, which is her "Average Order Size" or "Average Selling Price (ASP)." Now that we have those figures, we now can gauge how many appointments Sara will need to complete this year to have a solid chance of beating her year-end goal.

If we break $1 million down to a monthly sales number, Sara will need to average $83,000 per month in sales. With a $3,000 average selling price, she will need to sell 28 units per month to hit that number. To assess how many meetings with clients that will take, we divide her 60% closing ratio into the number of sales, and realize she needs to complete 46 appointments per month to achieve her monthly goal, on average. Eight of the calendar months contain four selling weeks, and four of them contain five selling weeks. During the four-week months she will need to complete 12 appointments per week, and during the five-week months, she will need to complete 10.

The great thing is, Sara can break these appointments up any way she likes. If she meets with clients every day, she needs to set a goal of two to three client appointments each day, for a total of 12. If she only wants to meet with new clients three days per week, she can adjust that and meet with 4 clients per day. If she decides to work with clients only two days a week (which I wouldn't recommend), that would mean she'd need to make six appointments each day.

	3-yr Average	Yearly Goal	Monthly Goal	Weekly Goal
Overall Sales	$773,000	$1,000,000	$83,333	$20,833
# of Orders	258	333	28	7
ASP	$3,000	$3,000	$3,000	$3,000
# of Appts	429	555	46	12

You get the picture. By applying the Law of Averages to your yearly goal and utilizing averages that have been developed by that person over time, we can reasonably forecast what would be sold in a year based on a quantified activity level.

You may be saying to yourself, "But Bret, I'm new to my company, so I don't have those statistics on my results. How will LOA help me?"

You're right. If you're new, you don't have those averages on your own performance. However, the company has those averages, based on the past performance of other sales reps that are in your position. My recommendation would be to take the overall average of all the reps in the company, and use those numbers as your baseline until you have completed enough appointments where your sample size becomes large enough to forecast based off of your own results.

When you look at sales from this perspective, it becomes a lot more fun and, in many ways, it becomes a game that's much easier to win. When you set your goals in this manner, you'll realize there really isn't an unrealistic goal. However, there can be an unrealistic time frame for achieving a certain number. If your current skills and habits don't allow you to reach your goal in the time frame you currently desire, don't give up! It just means you need to increase your activity, improve your skill set, and maybe even adjust your attitude.

If you learn to use the law of averages, work your ass off, and consistently look to improve, your results will start to improve – exponentially.

Surround yourself with great mentors. Learn to connect well with others. Plan your work, and work that plan with diligence and discipline. Become a master at identifying, reaching, and influencing decision makers. Finally, improve your selling skills every day through both experience and the abundance of resources at your fingertips.

Most importantly, have a blast doing it. While sales can be unnerving at first, it is a fun process, and the better you get, the more fun and gratifying this industry will become for you.

Finally, I'd like to sincerely thank you for purchasing and reading this book, and allowing me to play a very small role in your sales success. My hope is that this book has provided information, insight, and motivation that you will take out and start using immediately.

You can read all the books you want and gather all the information you can, but if you don't implement it *immediately,* you will never see the benefits from those efforts. As Mark Lovas used to remind with this quote from the late Stephen Covey, "To know and not to do is really to not know."

I have confidence in you and believe that if you purchased this book and went to the effort to digest the information, you will do yourself the honor of putting these items into action immediately.

Sales is a fun process. There's no other occupation or career like it. It's an extreme challenge, and some days it feels impossible. However, there's no feeling like making a sale, knowing you created that result, and knowing the reason that customer will benefit from your product or service for years is because of you.

So, find a great product to sell and a great company to represent, work your tail off, learn from experience, seek to improve every day, have a can-do attitude, and don't forget to have fun. If you do those things, you will enjoy a great career and create financial abundance for yourself and your family. Above all, you will have *The Selling Edge.*

"Great salespeople are not born or made. They evolve over time based on their dedication to excellence and their willingness to serve."
~ Jeffrey Gitomer

READING LIST

Cold Calling Techniques (That Really Work!) – by Stephan Schiffman

Emotional Intelligence – by Daniel Goleman

Givers Gain: The BNI Story – by Ivan Misner, PhD

How to Win Friends and Influence People – by Dale Carnegie

Love is the Killer App – by Tim Sanders

Networking Like a Pro: Turning Contacts into Connections – by Ivan Misner, PhD

Secrets of Closing the Sale – by Zig Ziglar

See You at the Top – by Zig Ziglar

The 5 Love Languages – by Gary Chapman

The Likeability Factor – by Tim Sanders

The Little Red Book of Selling – by Jeffrey Gitomer

The Power to Get In – by Michael Boylan

The Sales Bible – by Jeffrey Gitomer

The Tao of Twitter: Changing Your Life and Business 140 Characters at a Time – by Mark Schaefer

ABOUT THE AUTHOR

After starting his sales career with twelve straight unsuccessful sales meetings and no referrals to work with, Bret Barrie was discouraged. But deep down, he knew this world of sales couldn't be as impossible as it felt. Despite his friends advising him to ditch sales and get a "normal" job, Bret was determined to find success in sales. Using the strategies and tactics outlined in this book, Bret quickly catapulted himself into his company's Hall of Fame and earned multiple awards, including the President's Club Award. Throughout his career, Bret has shared these strategies with thousands of others, many of whom have reached the top in their respective industries. Today, Bret leads a top-producing sales team in the ultra-competitive medical device industry. In his spare time, he enjoys spending time with his wife and three children, working out, reading, writing, and playing baseball.

 Bret can be reached at:

bret@bretbarrie.com
Twitter: @BretBarrie
LinkedIn:www.linkedin.com/in/bretbarrie